Not Just a Mummy
Author Clare Bowers

Copyright © Clare Bowers 2018
All rights reserved

"Sometimes when you pick up your child you can feel the map of your own bones beneath your hands, or smell the scent of your skin in the nape of his neck. This is the most extraordinary thing about motherhood - finding a piece of yourself separate and apart that all the same you could not live without."
— Jodi Picoult, Perfect Match

Content

A Mother's Identity

This is Me

The Fear of the Unknown

Getting Trapped Under the Cover of Motherhood

Mummy Guilt

The Single Mum Who Made It

A Mother's Purpose

Anxiety is Not the Same as Fear

Mummy Time vs Me Time

The Mindful Mum

The Active Mum

You Don't Have to Change!

Mini Meltdown for Me

Picture Perfect, well almost!

Friendships

Finding Myself

Extending the family

What will they think?

Losing control

Look at Me

Relationships

Work Life for Mum

A School Run Mum

Routine and Focus

Money, Money, Money

I Can't Do Everything!

Seriously, Did They Say That?

Escape from the Daily Routine

Don't Forget About You

Moving Forward

A Mum with a Plan

Welcome Back

Special Thank You

A Mother's Identity:

Becoming a mother can be overwhelming. You're blessed with a life other than your own to protect, nurture and flourish. Subconsciously you can slip into the routine that naturally comes along with motherhood, focusing solely on your children and forgetting about your own needs.
That is what happened to me.

I live for my children. I would do everything in my power to protect them, but for a period of my own parenting journey I forgot who I was, and I'm not talking baby brain. I couldn't think my own thoughts without my mummy ones powering through. I would find myself sitting in silence because the children were taking naps, wondering what I needed to get ready for when they woke. Sometimes these thoughts came over and over, like waves crashing onto the shore. This was natural because my children's needs have, and always will, come before my own, which to me is unconditional parenting. However, I began to miss Clare, the business woman, friend, loving wife and individual.

I realised that my life, although I loved it, had become a case of mistaken identity. I had defined myself as, 'Just a Mummy', when there was a lot more about me than that. And society's view, that every aim and achievement of a woman is linked to how they are as a mother, had encouraged this.

The more I talk about my motherhood journey, and not feeling quite like me within this, the more women I meet who are feeling the same. These are the women who want to find their own identity and not the one society has created for what 'it' thinks a mother's role, ambition and daily life should be. I felt that society, meaning the people around me and the media with its political and cultural influences, had an expectation for me as a young, single mum to either fail or struggle.

It seems obvious when I reflect on this, but I wish I could go back and tell myself: Of course you feel like you're living a different identity when starting the motherhood journey - your body, your clothes, your mind, your priorities, they've all changed.

What I experienced wasn't something abnormal. This was real and raw. It was a massive learning curve for me, even if it did come years later and not at the time where it would have benefited me to know more. But I can share my knowledge here.

I never look back and regret any of my past experiences; that was my path and it taught me so many new lessons. But I want to tell mothers and women across the world, that it's okay to be you. Everything you feel and experience makes you who you are. Never forget the hard times, no matter how much they still may hurt, they are a massive part of your journey. They can fill you with the determination and empowerment to push you towards reaching all of your dreams and goals. You've got to believe in yourself. No one else can do this but you. I know you want this, as much as I want it for you.

It is true that you can buy the pram that you've been saving up for, get the nappies and externally prepare yourself for a baby. But you can't buy a preparation kit for your body and mind. This is an area that needs constant attention, and one that can go unnoticed during pregnancy and the early days of motherhood.

There is a way around this. I've found that to focus on a 'Must do for Mum' list is a way to get ready for this big change. You can choose what advice you want to take from people and also listen to your own intuition to make up this list.

After all, everyone in your life will have an opinion to how you should parent. The experience and advice that family, friends and even strangers will share with you, is from their own experiences. So, please take their words as advice and guidelines, not as your own personal instruction manual on how to be a mother.

If we live through other people's words, then our lives wouldn't be our own personal journeys. We wouldn't get to experience the everyday joys that make us thankful of who we are and what life has blessed us with. What makes you happy, won't necessarily make the person next to you happy, and what comes easy to you, might be a struggle for others. Most of the time we don't even know when our advice is coming across as a little too pushy. It's about being an active listener for another mother, which will benefit her, not to try and fix things with our own experiences.

Buying this book identifies the start of your own journey. Let me take you back to the beginning of mine.

This is Me

What already feels like so long ago, there was a young woman who lived her life to the full. Her only priorities were for herself and her career. The girl woke up, casually picked her clothes for the day ahead, and carefully applied her make-up. Public transport brought peace and relaxation as she sat with her own thoughts.

Little did the young woman know that her whole world was going to change, and she would find times when she didn't recognise herself or her own thoughts.

This book was created from my real experiences as a new mum, single mum, working mum, stay at home mum, business mum, a loving wife and a very rewarding ending.

I haven't held back with my thoughts, feelings and confessions, even though at times I did hesitate. But I truly believe that we can find ourselves instinctively holding back from the fear of being judged, discriminated against and not liked.

I couldn't imagine opening up and talking about my worries, fears and weaknesses when I first became a mother. But three children and my own business later, I feel I can encourage other mothers to open up and not fall victim to what they're told motherhood should look, sound and behave like.
You don't need to have the tidiest of homes, wear your hair perfect every day, speak about only the positive side to motherhood and you don't have to behave like you have nothing else in the world that you would like to achieve. It's okay not to mirror other mothers and it's okay to get it wrong sometimes; we're all human. Everything in my own journey, from being a Royal Navy engineer fixing gas turbines to a single mum changing nappies, happened to create the reason and experience that I needed to be able to write this book.

Hopefully I can support so many wonderful women and mothers across the world who are feeling trapped in an identity that is unfamiliar to them.
I refer to the word identity multiple times. I want you to understand that before I had my children, my identity was solely me, Clare. I had my first son at a young age of twenty. I thought becoming a mother had taken away a piece of my own identity. In reality, and what I have mindfully accepted now, having all three of my children didn't take anything away from my own identity, like I was led to believe and made to feel by outside influences.

It was often simple conversations that stayed with me. Moments like when I was attending my first midwife appointment and I was told by a lady in the waiting room that my hair looked nice, but I wouldn't have time to do it when the baby came. She said that new mums don't get time to do anything they want to. It felt like even the small things, like spending time on my appearance, would be taken away from me.

I wish I had known then that my children would add to my identity in a beautiful and powerful way, and that I would still have time for me. But for a period of my motherhood journey I was so clouded with negativity and listening to what others thought, that I nearly missed out on so many beautiful opportunities for me and my family.

Using my own experience to help support other women is one of the most rewarding gifts I could have ever imagined possessing. I want my readers to appreciate just how amazing you all are when you allow yourselves to 'just be you'.

We all have different roles throughout our lives. Sometimes we are career driven and other times we focus on raising a family, most of the time it's both simultaneously, but no matter what role you choose to take, this shouldn't define you as a person or change your identity. Yes, all these roles will lead you down different paths, some not being as easy to walk down as others, but that shouldn't stop us.

I like to think of these paths like this; if one path has more stones on than the other and begins to hurt your feet, what should you do? Put on suitable shoes, right? If one path is full of cold and rain what should you do? Wrap up and use an umbrella, right? So now that you have that mindset ask yourself if your life gets a bit tougher, what should you do? The answer for me would be to protect and shield myself, do you agree?

For me a life of teaching would have been wonderful. I enjoyed being around children so much and a part of me wanted to take the next steps from being a teaching assistant and gain the qualifications needed to have my own class. But in reality, it wasn't the right time for me when this opportunity came up. Instead I made the decision to return home every night, as I had a long commute and was a single mum with two young children. I'm not saying it isn't possible, but I didn't have the belief in my own identity at the time to make the changes for this to happen. I felt that I couldn't ask for help and that I would be judged for spending time on my hair, never mind further education and a new career.

Now, ten years later, I'm walking down both paths of career and family. I run a household, three children and a business. I've got the support from my husband, family and my friends and grab this help with both hands when and if needed. Situations change and that allows you to see opportunities more clearly. I want to tell you that just because you don't think you can do something now, doesn't mean you can't ever do it. You never know what opportunities are waiting for you around each corner.

Protecting yourself from the negativity that life brings with it doesn't for a second mean hiding away. You can protect yourself whilst standing on the frontline by using your voice. Using your words and behaviour choices mindfully will open up new opportunities for you to flourish.

Chapter One

The Fear of the Unknown

"All my worries about everything I didn't know kept building up when I was pregnant making me irrational and all over the place. I was like a child after eating a bag of Haribo or a lollipop - completely uncontrollable and knocking anything that gets in their path into space heights - but without the buzz or enjoyment." Amy

Have you ever experienced the overwhelming sensation that you aren't good enough for anyone, including yourself? I believe that any mother can feel like this when they find out they're pregnant, whether it's their first or fifth child. Each time is like being a new mum, because you never know quite what to expect, and it's this fear of the unknown that can affect all of us, if we allow it to.

Even just those words written down 'fear of the unknown', can invite irrational thoughts to race around our minds. The 'what if' factor of every unknown scenario of motherhood was a frequent visitor to my mind. All of those thoughts build up, overtaking any rational ones trying to calm us down.

I've read so many times in magazines, online, in pamphlets and in shared posts on social media that even the most knowledgeable and experienced professionals agree that when it comes to pregnancy, childbirth and motherhood there is still so much we can learn as a society. Opening ourselves up to every opinion and claimed fact that crosses our screens, papers and hospital notes can leave all women feeling very vulnerable, not to mention confused. Is it any wonder we question ourselves? I questioned myself every time I saw a new mum smiling from a magazine article and looking physically fit in what seemed like days after giving birth. Was I happy enough? Was I lazy?
But I learned to look in the right places.

There are lots of opinions of what motherhood should look like, and what you should be experiencing. I find the more the years go on, the more information can sound like it's turning into opinions, so I no longer felt like I had to believe everything I read. I even found supportive influences that took away my fear.

When I first became a mother, things were slightly different. I had my first two children before the internet became what it is today, and scarily before any social media platforms or many relatable pregnancy and parenting books were available on the shelves. Sometimes I think I'm lucky that I didn't have those influences, but then I feel that I missed out on the choice of support and knowledge that new mothers are getting now. Those first two times, I was dependent on the knowledge of the professionals who surrounded my pregnancy, my birth and the first years of motherhood. Yes, family members and friends gave me their advice, but it was always clouded with the positives, so that they didn't scare me. My mum would remind me that she would be there for me every step of the way because I would need all the support I could get. It was so lovely to feel supported but of course in my head I was thinking, wow is it going to be that hard that I need so much assistance? My mum has always kept to her word through the good times and the tough times. I appreciated that at the time and looking back it makes me smile because of how much of the reality of motherhood she sheltered me from before I began my journey.

I often meet women who feel claustrophobic from all the advice that is shared with them, and I also meet mothers who wish they had support like that. They all feel lonely, unseen and unheard. The pain and confusion of these women is real and it's probably happening to someone close to you.

Recently I read that 1 in 5 women experience post-natal depression, which can be linked to pregnancy experiences. Support can be on the doorstep but yet so far to reach out to. So, what causes this fear that mothers are experiencing? Where does it come from and why doesn't it leave when asked? I believe that my fear came from my own thoughts. I built up this image of what people would say if I asked for support. I repeated the responses I would receive inside my head. I was scared of not knowing what people were going to think or say to me.

Most of the fears I had when pregnant with all three of my children came from the areas that I wasn't too sure about, that everyone else seems to have an opinion on, even though all of their views would just make me even more confused. I needed direct answers to my questions, but everything seemed to have an 'if or but' added to it.

I wanted to hear real life experiences from new mums; where did they go for support if they needed it? Were there any mums' groups I could join? I didn't have anyone to ask, so I would visit my local library to see if there were any updates on the local board. I wanted to know if I had to bottle feed or could I breastfeed? I asked my midwife and she told me to try and see how I felt about it, but how would I know what felt right?

I soon realised I had to figure motherhood out for myself and learn as I went on. I could change nappies and feed on demand, my babies were healthy and happy, and so I was always given the thumbs up at weigh-ins and doctor appointments.

But from my first child to my third, the changes in advice changed dramatically. I felt as if I had slept in a bubble for ten years and not heard of any of the recent scares doing the rounds. Everyone would comment on how things have changed and how I couldn't do what I did in the past. I was just at the stage of my parenting where I thought I was a pretty good mum, and now I was finding my identity being shaped into an insecure mum. I would look at my older children wondering how they were even standing, as I had made up the bottles in the mornings for the day which you're told not to do now. When I would ask what had changed, no one seemed to know the answer. I was even frightened about my third child having a dummy because I read on social media pages that it was linked to delayed speech.

I took all of the new advice in, but would try and protect the mother I had been to my two older children, by reminding the professionals, friends and family members that I had birthed before. I found myself questioning if this was how society was treating all new mothers now? I understand there are facts that need to be shared by professionals, of course there are. However, there are also ways of educating new mothers without them feel belittled or creating fear around their choices.

Within some parenting groups I visited, there would be people who thought that by pushing their own guidelines, experiences and education onto the others, they could assert their identities amidst this confusion. But then the other expectant or new mums were feeling defined by how they parented against all this information rather than who they were. As I was losing who I was too, I would sit back and stay quiet.

I wish I had stood my ground, but when you're unsure of who you are, you don't want to be noticed.

It wasn't until the birth of my third baby, that I started to voice my thoughts around pregnancy, parenting and life. I now question any advice and give suggestions on what I think would be beneficial to both myself and my children.

I learnt a valuable lesson. You can be told 50 different ways on what you will feel during pregnancy, birth and motherhood, and all 50 of these opinions can be wrong. Only your unique journey will determine the experience you have. Listen to the opinions of those close to you but never forget that you have the last say; you are in control no matter how out of control you can feel. Don't ever lose sight of that; ask the questions, talk to the professionals, but share your opinions and beliefs and most importantly believe in yourself. If something doesn't feel right, ask again and again and bring your own opinions and intuition into it too.

Chapter Two

Getting Trapped Under the Cover of Motherhood

"I wasn't aware in the first few years of becoming a mum, that everything I was feeling wasn't healthy. I just thought this was motherhood." Kayleigh

Pregnancy is a time where you can respect your body for giving you such a precious gift, a new life. It can also become a very lonely journey. The days can seem like weeks and the weeks like years, while the kindness of a stranger asking you how long you have left can dramatically turn into a repeated annoyance, even though people's intentions are to uplift and excite you. Hormones are high, and emotions are even higher. One minute you're loving everything about your pregnancy and then suddenly without any warning, you can start to feel the overwhelming tears and confusion creeping in. Within the blink of an eye you're in a dark place, unsure on how you ended up there, and having no voice to guide you.

This sense of fear can take over your whole experience, and leave you feeling low and cautious of every move you make. It's far from a pretty sight and can become uncomfortable to witness, even in the closest of relationships. It can have a negative effect on your wellbeing, making you feel uneasy and on edge.

This can happen in the most content of pregnancies and early days of motherhood. My third baby was planned and excitingly expected, but I still had plenty of days where I wanted to hide from the world under my duvet and shut my family out. I was sick from the sixth week, like I was with my previous pregnancies.

I used to feel selfish admitting this, but I missed all of the things I hadn't appreciated before I became a mother, when I was pregnant with my first child. I reminisced a lot about the times I had before I became a mother, doing the things I enjoyed as a woman, like meeting friends for food and deep, meaningful conversations. At one stage in my first pregnancy, I thought I had lost this 'Me Time' forever. I couldn't get out the house as much due to the sickness. I hardly had a social life because I didn't have the energy to make the effort.

I was serving in the Royal Navy at the time I became pregnant with my first child and waiting to be discharged. I had the world at my feet. I could do as I pleased when I pleased. I was so young and naive. Naive enough to believe that motherhood wouldn't change my world that much; it would just increase my happiness, right? I was right about my happiness increasing; it went through the roof! But it was also overwhelming, especially when the sickness started taking away that 'do what I like when I like' attitude.

My little boy, who is now twelve years old, turned my world upside down. I adored him as soon as I held him in my arms and I knew that this little man was going to impact me a lot more than I had originally thought. You know that feeling, the one that takes your breath away, that suddenly puts your whole life into perspective and brings reason to your every moment. This is when your identity can grow and complement motherhood, instead of slipping under the covers of nappies, hourly feeds and baby talk. But it can be difficult to get to this point. I was overwhelmed with emotions and I remember writing out my shopping list thinking how different it looked compared to before I became a mum. Removing this cover of fear can be difficult, but it's not impossible. You're still in there, no matter how hard it is to see past the emotions. The first thing to recognise is that asking for help isn't a sign of failure or bad parenting; it's the opposite. You are strong for realising that you need help to get all of those bottled up feelings out at such a vulnerable time.

Think of the cover, and then think about the barriers that are holding you back from being true to yourself and finding your identity. We all have different barriers; mine ranged from childcare issues to fear of what people would think of me. Imagine a group of rocks. Each rock represents one of the barriers that you feel hold you back. Imagine the rocks being placed around your cover, holding it down. Step by step you need to find your own way of lifting one rock up at a time, slowly and at your own pace. It's not a race; if it was it wouldn't work.

The people around you can help you lift those rocks with their words and their actions, if you let them. Talking about these barriers will make the rocks feel lighter, light enough for you to lift the cover of fear. Reading self-help blogs and books and watching inspirational films will also allow you to see that you're not alone and there is always someone out there who is willing to help you, or ways you can support yourself through even the most demanding situations.

Looking back to that first pregnancy, I wish that I had found the confidence to speak out to the people around me and get some help to remove the rocks.

This might be more difficult if, for whatever reason, your pregnancy may not be what you expected. My sickness left me feeling like a stranger to my children and family. I felt worthless because I could no longer be as organised. The house had derailed and so had I.

There is an overwhelming feeling of being unsure about everything. This takes its toll, and you can't think straight, let alone guide yourself into motherhood, all singing and dancing.

That's when you need to stop and take a breath, and okay here's your warning; you're possibly going to cry … But that's fine. Sit back and think about the present moment, how are you feeling? Let those tears flow because we've all been there. If you can write these feelings down, and feel comfortable with keeping a log, you can look back on the early days of pregnancy and see how far your mind and body does overcome through this experience. It's pretty amazing. "Make the most of it before the baby comes." That's something else you'll have in your mind that can feel overwhelming, as so many people will say it.

I know it's said without an intention to scare or cause worry to a new mother, but it can plant seeds of worry. The last thing an expectant mother needs to hear from family, friends and even strangers is that her life is about to massively change and the things she is doing in the present may not be acceptable or even doable when her new born arrives. This sets off an identity crisis as you start to question how the current 'you' will fit in with this big change.

And yes, your life is going to change, you know that, and everyone around you who has become a parent or a legal guardian to a baby or child knows the impact too. However, this doesn't have to be a negative thing. You just need to remember that focusing on yourself isn't selfish.

Your environment and wellbeing during pregnancy is a key priority. Don't feel guilty about this, as your growing baby's health will be a focus within this too.

I understand that keeping your eye on what's going on in your life over the lives of those around you can be pretty challenging. Sometimes it feels like you must put blinkers on, as they do with horses to keep them focused on the road ahead, but it doesn't have to be like that. You can help yourself stay focused by writing daily affirmations, creating a vision board for yourself and writing to do lists. This always helped me.

You should not have to worry about the whispers of the confusing and negative conversations that tend to get stuck in your mind. Build a protective layer with a strong mindset to keep your thoughts as your own.

Chapter Three

Mummy Guilt

"I experienced a horrendous amount of bullying growing up, especially in school. I was made to believe I was the worst person in the world through the words and behaviour of others around me. I would tell myself I was too fat to eat chips or too ugly to have a boyfriend, no one would ever except me or love me. I now know through a lot of counselling and self-help groups that I'm allowed to love myself for who I am and not from who I was made to feel I was." Gina

No matter how big society or influencers around you might say the impact of becoming a mother will be, we all deal with this in different ways. But one thing we all have in common is guilt. Let's get to the core of where all this guilt stems from and dive into what impact social pressures, imagery and daily situations have on your mind, sometimes without you even noticing.

The fear of failure is already embedded in our minds, as we grow up in a society that tells us daily if we are winners or losers.

At school, we get the questions and tasks that are asked of us either right or wrong. We are marked from local standards set by previous students in our areas, and national benchmarks. There has never been the opportunity to set our own achievements, unique to each of us.

Throughout school I wasn't even close to achieving what was expected, so I didn't push myself in fear of even more failure. I was gliding along, and as dramatic as this may sound to you, I felt like I was always waiting for something inside me or someone around me to show me what my purpose was. For anyone who experienced a tough time socially or academically at school, it's hard not to feel insecure and powerless in the real world, even with the school's best intentions behind you. It's scary just how much self-doubt and lack of confidence comes down to school life, a time when education should be the focus of each day. Sadly, school years are not always plain sailing. The words and actions of others, just like in adulthood, can have a massive impact on the amount of belief and confidence you have in yourself.
I believe that this insecurity of not meeting the standards society sets carries over into motherhood. But you can turn this into a positive identity.

The women I meet who experienced bullying during school are always willing to open up about the challenges and barriers this created for them during school life, in adulthood, and especially in motherhood. They all agree that the bullying added an extra layer of protection that now covers their children throughout their lives. They are now powerful, strong and confident women who can stand up for what they believe in.

Learning to accept that the behaviour of those around you belong to them and not to your mind is powerful, and can shift your thinking from negative into positive. The memories you have will always be hurtful, but the guilt surrounding them can be lifted when you no longer blame yourself. You can awaken to the understanding that it wasn't anything that you deserved for being true to who you are.

Social media is a fantastic resource, but what it's doing to some women across the world is without a doubt, a massive form of social torture. The daily scrolling through the thoughts, behaviour and actions of other people can bring to light that 'I'm doing something wrong' feeling. You can find yourself thinking negative thoughts and directing them at certain people and their posts, often for no reason at all. It's poisoning our minds. I once sat thinking that if I put a picture up of my new car everyone was going to think I was boasting about my life, and guess what I didn't post it. Instead I scrolled through releasing that negative energy onto everyone else's posts.

That wasn't me; what was I turning into? I was behaving in a way that wasn't natural to who I was inside. I would see mothers enjoying their 'Me Time' and I would automatically think badly of them for leaving their babies! What was wrong with me? Why couldn't a hard-working mother go out with her friend without being criticized. I hated myself for feeling so bitter towards other women's choices. My identity was now shaped by resentment.

I didn't want to be labelled as the woman who, just because she doesn't understand a choice that another mother makes, automatically thinks it to be a negative. To get myself back to who I knew I was, I needed to examine why I was feeling like this.

I started to read different magazines, looking for some guidance. They were filled with gorgeous women who had managed to get back their beach body sizes within a few weeks of having their babies, or stunning mothers who lay next to their adorable sleeping bundles of joy. This was while I sat nursing my baby who wouldn't sleep for more than an hour. I would then read contrasting articles on how women were overweight and struggling with motherhood. There were also endless ones featuring celebrity mothers who were all supposedly struggling to lose the baby weight. They couldn't cope with the lack of sleep that new babies bring with them and their relationships were all in ruins because of the new responsibilities that came with parenting.

Something wasn't adding up with me. How could these magazines get away with making women feel like rubbish? These images and stories were having a massive impact on the way I thought I should look, feel and what a mother should look like. I was the opposite of that glossy picture, so was I doing it wrong?

Body-shaming articles and the pressure that comes with being a new mother need to stop before they cause any more damage. But they never will and it's because it all comes down to profit. Magazines know that if they put a front cover of a celebrity not looking her best, other women will relate and purchase the issue as way of trying to cope with their own insecurities.

It seems obvious now that I was envious about the freedom of my own choices, like what I was doing over the weekend and how much sleep I was going to have that night, while I was reading about these mothers. But then I recognised that this was being controlled from the outside by society through social media, magazines and TV.
But we don't need these barriers and we can block them.

One remark about your choice in clothing or behaviour can knock your confidence down to a level where it's hard to pick it up. I was told that I dressed more like an older mum, which made me question what the difference was? And who decided what a young mum should be wearing compared to an older mother?

You need to start questioning if these views define who you are and what you can achieve in your life. They shouldn't, but try telling that to the lady sitting on her own in a room filled with people confidently enjoying themselves and celebrating life, who throughout her life has been told that she will never amount to anything. She believes the words of others because they power through her own thoughts, and to react against them she needs energy. Sadly, those people took her physical and mental energy from her through an endless amount of nights crying into her pillow, blaming herself for all of the negative energy she attracts towards her from a guilt that she can't let go of. If you could give one piece of advice to this woman, what would it be? Mine was to let go and look within.

But how did I get through this personality transformation that I was experiencing which was overshadowed by the guilt of not feeling good enough?

As you can imagine, to challenge every thought can be physically draining, not to mention how mentally exhausting it is for your mind to dive into every thought in detail, and then analyse it. I began to drown in my own thoughts, and I had to stop this before I sent myself crazy. I needed support. And in fact, it was one of the very things that had turned me that way, which ended up helping me become myself again.

I turned social media into my saviour and chose more empowering magazines and books. This guided me into positive, happy thoughts. I found the right online identity I needed through the right groups and communities, which allowed me to start putting back the pieces of who I was. I started talking to like-minded women who fuelled me with inspiration and gave me acceptance.

I took a stand and decided that I would read more positivity, talk more positively, defend my thoughts from negativity and create the right environment that would fuel my identity as Clare.

If Clare is strong, mindful and aware, then that means as a mother I was setting a visibly positive example for my children.

Chapter Four

The Single Mum Who Made It

"I didn't have the choice when I became single whilst pregnant. My partner at the time walked away and I couldn't force him to stay so I allowed him to keep on walking. My pregnancy was beautiful but there were times when I felt so alone especially when watching couples who were excited together in the hospital waiting areas. I had to stay strong for myself and my unborn baby and I'm proud to say with the support of my family I did." Zara

I've met so many mothers who are raising their children alone, either through a mutual agreement, bereavement or reasons beyond their control. I know how hard it can be not to have someone to talk to. And society doesn't always make it easy. I was listening to the radio in the car one morning when the presenter mentioned how children who were being raised by a 'lone parent' scored noticeably lower in their exam results. This hit me hard.

My mum and dad had divorced when I was young and now I was questioning my own upbringing and that of my own children's as I had been a single mum too. Both of them were doing well, and despite not being seen as 'academic' by the school system, I was running a successful business. I asked a couple of mothers for their thoughts and we all agreed that it's not about your relationship status; it's more about the amount of support that you receive throughout your whole education, both from school and from home. Support ideally should come in the form of encouragement from both parents, but this is pretty challenging if you are no longer in a relationship together.

If you've been through a tough break up and then you are asked to put the words co-parenting and communication into the same sentence you can automatically jump to the conclusion that it's not possible. Sometimes it isn't, but if you both want it then you can make it work. I don't have to communicate with my ex-partner now because my children are old enough to have their own mobile phones and we have a clear set time and day routine and that works for us as a family.

When I asked women who had also raised children alone who they turned to, many replied how they would find themselves talking to their baby bumps about their day, and about how excited they were to bring their precious child into the world which helped them to refuel their energy and positive thinking. That is not only precious, but also shows how powerful a woman's mind is. To convert all of the insecurities they were feeling about becoming a single parent into love is magical and truly inspiring.

The feelings that can come with being a single mum like loneliness, anxiety and fear of not being accepted can start to affect you from the moment you walk into the hospital for your first appointment, through to the birthing room and all of the baby groups attended.

I would feel nervous when anyone asked me about my children's father. I was embarrassed, and I wish I could time-hop and whisper in my ear that it was okay and I had nothing to fear.

I lied so many times when I was a single parent. I even remember buying myself a dress ring to wear when attending groups just so I wasn't approached or questioned about my marital status! How crazy does that even sound? I didn't feel that I could be who I truly was. I couldn't embrace the fact that I was raising two children and I was doing a good job at it! I wish I could go back and tell that to myself when I was alone at the registration of my first baby.

I had severe morning sickness called Hyperemesis Gravidarum throughout all of my pregnancies. As no one else could experience this with me, I reached out to health professionals. It's a difficult illness to explain and treat, so I even started to think it was my own fault that I felt like this. I was in and out of hospital for hydration. None of the other mums could make conversation because they were also very ill. This started my motherhood journey off in a very isolated way.

It's true when they tell you that depression, anxiety and fear can make you feel that you're standing alone in a crowded room. In my case, I was in a crowded hospital.

With my first child, the guilt of being in hospital wasn't so bad because nobody needed me at home, but with my second child, it was the opposite. With a small gap of one year and twelve days, let's just say there were times I questioned if I should just move us all into the hospital. I would cry just before they would take my samples. This is because I knew the results would mean I had to leave my son for the night to stay over in a hospital bed, hooked up to a drip with no conversation. I knew it was the best for my unborn child and I appreciate all of the hard work the hospital staff delivered for me, but that didn't take away the guilt every time I had to leave my son. I would lie there wondering where he thought I had gone, as he was too young to understand.

By my third child, I decided to try and take more control as I didn't want the identity of 'sick mum' and for the loneliness to define me again. I took medication, despite my worries about the side-effects. Medication isn't for everyone, but it was my way out.

I wasn't going to allow this pregnancy to take control of my life and take time away from my children, not to mention work! I hadn't even told them I was pregnant yet after achieving a new role supporting children with additional social, emotional and behavioural needs. I didn't want them to simply see me as a 'sick mum'.

Alongside the medication, I forced myself out of bed and to exercise gently.

I carried a few sick bags wherever I went so that I didn't embarrass my two older children by throwing up here, there and everywhere. Did it make me feel amazing? No, it didn't. However, spending time with my older children out in the open did make me feel like a good mum. It also helped me to feel less isolated.

If you have suffered with sickness during pregnancy, then you will know there isn't much to stop it. Don't be too hard on yourself.

In addition to the sickness, during my third pregnancy, I was worried about the large age gap. I wasn't naive to the fact that baby number three was going to stir things up in our house.

But I had grown up and experienced so much in the ten year gap of having my oldest to my newborn. Despite this, and the fact that I was now in a strong relationship with someone who loved me for who I was and listened to me, I was still carrying the same fears that I had the first time. Would my baby be okay? Would my relationship survive the sleepless nights and the 'no time to talk, let alone cuddle nights'? What would happen to the older kids' times with me? Would the new baby allow that? Or would I spend my time apologising?

In the end my children answered all this for me. They formed a powerful bond with their new little sister. They understood her needs and helped out as much as they could. They adored her. My worries faded…I wasn't alone.

Chapter Five

A Mother's Purpose

"I found that when I became a mum at 16 years old the people around me would pity me and there weren't many congratulations because in their view that was it for me; I was now a mum and my sole focus was raising my child, not being a young woman. Little did they know that becoming a mum empowered me to want more from my life." Nicola

Whether you're a single mum or not, the same insecurities can creep in slowly like a poison when you find yourself with a new identity as a parent. You can start to question if there is a point. I'm here to tell you that there isn't a point, there's a purpose.

All our purposes are unique to our personalities, experiences, values and lives. My purpose during my low times was always my children. I wanted them to look up to me as a loving mother who would move the earth for them and stop at nothing to create a path for them to flourish on.

This hasn't always come easy. I don't think it ever will either. During pregnancy and early motherhood, my own thoughts, views and opinions didn't really exist. But I was always on time for school pick-up, packed lunches were always done and my effort in work would never go unnoticed. However, all of the things in life that I prioritised didn't include any of my own needs, and I didn't even realise that I was slowly letting myself disappear. What was my purpose?

I was being praised for my excellent time-keeping, organisational skills, the children's behaviour, attendance in school and how I made motherhood look so natural. I didn't see notice the barriers I was creating for myself. When you're experiencing the same routine day in day out, it's hard to think about yourself. Your children are happy and everyone around you is happy; you assume that you have to accept the life you have. Why wouldn't you want to? It was perfect to everyone looking in. You'll seem ungrateful if you complain, right?

If you feel that speaking out about your feelings is complaining, then that's your first barrier. Never feel like you can't raise a voice for your own needs.
Personally, I think that society has created these images of the perfect woman that are now expected to come with motherhood. It's as though our purpose has become to compete with each other.

One image you've got is the mother who's not afraid to show her real feelings and emotions during pregnancy and throughout parenting. She's strong, powerful and embraces motherhood. She's very strong and stands up for her own rights as a mother and she's not afraid of who hears or questions her.

Another image you've got is a mother who also embraces motherhood but in her own style, choosing to keep this to herself. You don't hear her complain about motherhood or life in general, she gets on with her daily to do list and would rather not get involved in any discussions that might cause conflict.

Within the two you can get a mother who cooks fresh meals every night and another who admits that she relies on oven food due to time restraints and fussy children. Then you might have a mother who never allows TV, compared to one who relies on it so that the children are occupied while she gets things done.

It sounds like they could clash. But then I realised that is only because society made me think they would, through social media articles and magazines setting these different types of mothers up against each other.

Both of these images of motherhood should be seen as role models. They have the same goal and purpose - to love, empower and inspire their children.

Having another mother as a role model can inspire and raise you up on even the lowest of days. There are so many women I look up to, both in my family and in my community. These women are strong, powerful and very honest. I admire their willingness to show the world the real images of motherhood, helping to reduce the expectations that new mothers are being challenged with.

Chapter Six

Anxiety is Not the Same as Fear

"With there being very little antenatal care in my community I began to feel frustrated that the care needed was coming either too late or not at all. My frustration turned into a realisation that I had to do something to help support this crisis, that's when Beautiful New Beginnings was born with the ethos to support and empower parents on their parenting journey from birth." Carolyn

Until I was pregnant, I had never experienced intense anxiety. My eyes still well up when I think about the time that I did. I would feel silly talking about it then, because I couldn't make sense of my own mind. So I didn't breathe a word. I sat in silence and let the world pass me by, every day thinking that surely I should have been overjoyed that I was expecting my first child, but I was terrified, scared and very lonely. I became irritable, especially when I didn't understand something or hadn't had the best of sleep, because of the worries that raced through my mind. I kept going over and over what life with a baby was going to be like.

All this anxiety feels like it should be excitement. It's therefore one of the hardest things to talk about openly without feeling like the worst mother in the world, before you've even become one! This can affect your sleep patterns when you're pregnant. Thoughts of the upcoming birth and parenting guides is enough to give anyone sleepless nights.

Time was my particular enemy in the fight against anxiety. I was counting down the months, weeks and days until my due date, because obviously my baby was going to come on time, right? Wrong! I went over. Those days felt like years! I would call the midwife when I got a twitch, to be told to wait until my waters broke, or until I was in that much pain I had to come in. I was told, you'll just know when it's the real thing. But how would I know? This was my first baby.

The midwives know their role inside and out; I just didn't realise then that their calmness was necessary. After all, I wasn't the only woman in labour who needed their attention. But my anxiety took over and it felt like I was failing before my baby was even born. How didn't I know what real labour was? Of course the anxiety of not being good enough or knowing enough had been present throughout my pregnancy. Even though I was healthy, didn't smoke or drink and exercised regularly, I still felt like I wasn't doing enough or getting anything right.

Stories of miscarriages particularly played on my mind. Sitting in the hospital waiting room, booked in for my 20 week scan with my first born, I met a woman whose first pregnancy had ended in miscarriage. She was so nervous about her second. Although she walked out smiling and holding her new scan photo that day, I was shaken by what could happen to any woman.

I knew that I had to get out of this mindset. I needed to walk away from it all, so I did just that.

I would walk to work and family and friends' houses because I liked being out in the open air. It was the only time that I felt like I wasn't being judged for not knowing what I was doing or reading over stories that put me on edge. I would walk past strangers who didn't know my story and didn't see the confusion on my face because I would smile at them. Did they ever praise me for keeping healthy during pregnancy? This was a thought that struck me. It seemed to me like no one saw anything unless it was a negative.

I count my blessings that my babies were healthy. Many women across the world go through traumatic pregnancies, which can have lasting effects on their mental health and wellbeing. I still don't think there is enough support during pregnancy for this. There's an expectation for you to get on with it, especially if you've had previous children.

But every pregnancy experience can bring different anxieties. I think the best thing anyone, either a professional, friend, family member or stranger can do is to put themselves in the mother's shoes and get to know her. I understand this would be difficult for professionals because there doesn't seem to be enough time in the day for them, but it would be nice to have a more personal touch added to the wellbeing side of pregnancy.

Pregnancy looks and feels different for each woman, which is why more individualised support is needed. It's a precious experience for all mothers to go through, but it is part of you and therefore your individual identity and experience.

Chapter Seven

Mummy Time vs Me Time

"Talk about a whirlwind, my daughter arrived very early and very poorly. I spend the first 7 months beside my baby not moving to have a proper meal or an adult conversation. My dress size vanished, as did my identity. I was withering away inside and outside, but I wasn't missing a second with my daughter because I didn't know how long I had left with her. Three years later and I have a very happy, healthy toddler, which I'm extremely grateful for. However, because of the trauma we both suffered, I won't let her move out of my sight in fear of losing her. I haven't got an identity except for being a mother. I hope I eventually branch out and make new friendships to find me again. There have been so many times where I've written my children's names or dates of birth on forms that were meant for me. It's easily done when you're so used to writing about the children." Sarah

When I'm asked about the differences between 'Mummy Time' and 'Me Time', the truth is that what these two very different times mean to me, doesn't always resemble what they mean to other mothers. Again, it is all about individual identity. Mummy Time for me is not just when I'm with the children, but when I'm still doing mum related tasks and thinking in 'mum mode'. I find myself having quiet time and suddenly all of next week's school activities will jump into my mind, or when I am out having a cup of tea with friends and we end up talking about our children the whole time. Me Time can be when you are alone, or with your partner or friends, and can focus on you and what you enjoy. I like cinema dates with my husband a lot now and I don't feel guilty asking for a babysitter because I know we both deserve that time.

Being on your own can look lonely to a stranger, when it is a sanctuary for you. A perfect experience of this was when I was in a coffee shop and my toddler had fallen asleep. Even though the sensible mum thing to do would have been to use that opportunity to zoom around the shops and pick up the things I need, I rebelled. I sat with a hot chocolate and my own thoughts for what seemed like hours. I took one nice picture to prove to my friends that it is possible to get some peace and quiet even when you're a mum of three, then I put my phone away. I had to smile to myself when the lady beside us asked me if I wanted a magazine to read. I wondered if she had mistaken my peace for boredom.

An hour to yourself, with your own thoughts, can make such a massive difference to your wellbeing. Sitting on the couch at home while your baby sleeps or when the children are all in school, doesn't mean you're selfish or that your house is going to derail. It means you care enough about your own health, to stop and charge back up! Don't ever give up on your own needs, because they'll prepare you for when you hit the tough times.

As your children grow older you will find their needs in some areas grow, like in education, and in the other areas they become more independent, wanting to go out with friends and make their own breakfast. Use that independence to have the 'Me Time' that you deserve. If your little one is playing happily on the floor with her toys, open the book you've been wanting to read. Children need their own 'Me Time' too.

Trying to get the time out to spend working on building your identity back up when your children are young can be challenging. You know that you shouldn't be thinking about uniform and baby ballet when you're out enjoying yourself, but you will. The guilt that comes with 'Me Time' doesn't give up easily. Remind yourself that all mothers are allowed to feel happy when they're not with their children. It's healthy!

When I didn't have the Me Time I needed, I was overwhelmed with negative emotions that would make me question everything. This was because I couldn't fully be me during as I was still responding to everyone else's needs.

I have come so far after being in such a confusing place. This allows me to encourage other mothers. If I could have guilt-free Me Time, even when I was a single mum of two who suffered with anxiety, depression and loneliness, then it could happen for anyone.

There were reasons I didn't feel like I could have Me Time in the past. One was shame. My idea was to appear as though I never needed time to myself, so that people would think I was coping well and flying through motherhood. I already had so many statistics against me. I didn't want to prove them to be true.

But I had it all wrong. I still needed my own identity, found only through Me Time.

However, if I was asked to come to something without my children, the guilt and shame of looking like a bad mother for leaving them would stop me.

What I didn't realise at the time is how much I did miss being on my own and allowing myself to be one of the adults who could hold down a conversation without having to run around after my toddlers. You know that feeling when you're just getting deep into a topic that you enjoy, to having to exit without finishing because of something like a potty crisis or a dispute over a toy.

I also had the issue, like any mother, that I wanted to protect my children from anything that could cause them harm. Through this, I created barriers that became too high to be knocked down easily. And I was adding extra cement to them through my actions and behaviour.

For me, the loneliness that you experience being a single mum, and after your children have gone to sleep is a pretty hard experience to talk about. Having no one beside you to talk about your day to, and the genuine belief that no one but your children are thinking about you, does leave you feeling deflated and unwanted.

Of course it's not just single mums who can experience this. Some women who are in relationships can feel just as lonely if they haven't got the support of their partners.

I found myself making up excuses of why I couldn't go out that evening, or why I wasn't free for that birthday celebration. The truth is motherhood exhausted me. I put all of my energy into my children, and I forgot to save some for much needed time with my friends and with myself. This may come across as selfish, but it's true and common for a woman to crave that 'Me Time' that she once had. The stigma that is around this needs to change. It's causing women to feel unappreciated, unseen and unknown. These are all common feelings and behaviours of post-natal depression. I have seen the devastating effects on women I hold dear to me, strong women who for a second took their eye off their own wellness, and battled extremely difficult emotions which caused and left their own individual insecurities.

I needed a change. But we all know that when you're feeling so deflated it's easy to go with the flow and not challenge what is stopping you from taking the right action. I found that taking small action steps, allowed me to build up the mental strength needed to stick to a plan of action.

One of my first steps was to take that desired vision inside my mind and have it out on display every day. This would be my reminder of what I want and the changes I need to make.

I used this process after having my third child as I wanted to spend more time at home being a mum. I decided to create my own platform for women just like me, who wanted choices. That was when my business MUMBOSSUK was born. I celebrate women's successes, empowering them to focus on their own goals and helping them achieve this through my platform. This was the 'Me Time' I needed and it has changed my life and made me happy in my career and identity alongside motherhood.

After planning a realistic vision on how you can get your own 'Me Time' around motherhood and everyday life, you have to make it a priority. Yes that might sound unrealistic to you, but if that's how you're thinking now, you must need this time to happen. You can't run at such a high level and not give your mind and body the rest it deserves.

You're allowed to take time out when you need it. Even if it's a swipe through your social media, it's still connecting, and this is sometimes the only way mums can get their feelings and thoughts out. You automatically want to talk about your pregnancy or baby, that's normal, but try not to forget yourself. Did you enjoy your morning walk or trip to the hairdressers? Are you enjoying motherhood? Have you met up with friends? You're still human, motherhood should add to your identity, and not take it away.

Chapter Eight

The Mindful Mum

"I wake up every day and remind myself how excited I am for the opportunities that the day has in store for me. Just because they haven't presented themselves in a previous day it doesn't mean that they won't today." Katy

Mindfulness to me means living in the present moment and not allowing the past or the future to determine my choices. Being a mum of three has its benefits when it comes to supporting other mothers. I get asked about my experiences and how I manage my business around my family life. People want to know how I am always on time for everything. That's a life skill from my time in the Royal Navy! But I've used that to help other mums with their time-keeping by recommending diaries, planners and mindfulness courses.

One of the environment changes that I would have made before becoming a mother would be to introduce mindfulness into my home. I strongly believe that you can create a relaxing environment before your baby is born, to help both mum and newborn settle in. When everything around you is calm and relaxed, organisation and time-keeping becomes a lot easier.

I only reached out to the world of mindfulness during my third pregnancy. After delivering a session in my then workplace, I saw the positive impact it had. I hoped that it would help with all of the sickness and anxiety I was experiencing. It did immediately open my mind to just how much energy I was using worrying about possible scenarios and other people. I decided to make mindfulness a vital part of my routine, even if it was just one activity per day. It soon became natural to me and I relaxed enough to enjoy and be present during my pregnancy just that little bit more.

I didn't believe that I was capable of moving forward from past experiences like a relationship break-up and judgement from being a single mother. I didn't know then that by holding onto these negative memories, I was keeping them alive.

I allowed them to restrict the opportunities I went for in life, because I was frightened that those memories would repeat themselves in the present and I would experience the hurt and anger all over again.

But I worked through this.

I started small with mindfulness activities. I would play relaxing music while I was falling asleep.

I soon stepped it up a level and began to take my children out to parks, turn my phone on silent and walk in the present moment talking to them about what we could hear, smell and see, and how it made us feel. We once spent 15 minutes trying to see the bird we could hear in the tree branches above our head. It was magical as we were all in the same moment enjoying and recognising one another without being distracted by mobile phones, televisions and gaming stations.

It seemed to come more natural to my children than it did to me. As soon as I recommended that we practised mindfulness with our words and actions, they were all for it because they knew that it meant more activities where they got to spend time with their mum, whose focus was all about them.

I'm not suggesting that your focus isn't on your children if you don't do mindfulness, but it is easy to get distracted. This can be through work commitments, friends who call around just as you're sitting down for supper or when you're out as a family and your mobile rings. It happens a lot more than we realise. When you're mindful in your day to day life, you start to value the present moment and make the right changes in order to enjoy those precious times with your loved ones.

After a visit to the park with my youngest daughter who has just turned three, I wrote a post on social media to explain our experience. This got a lot of positive attention and other mums commented that they wanted to follow in my footsteps, switch off and focus on the present moment with their children.
Here is how the post read ...

Today was one of those mindful days where I enjoyed a coffee with friends and then took the afternoon off to enjoy a picnic with my daughter Aurora, who has just turned 3 years old.

I don't have any pictures other than this, as I only chose to take my phone out once to capture the whole day.

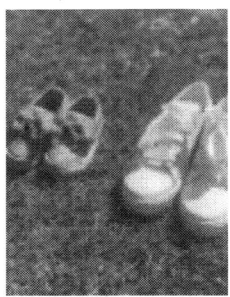

I bet at first glance you just see shoes ... and you're right. We took them off and we chased each other on the grass. We played airplanes and Aurora laughed uncontrollably and that's when it hit me. I had truly switched off from the outside world and I was present in that moment with my daughter. I didn't want to take lots of pictures to show the world that I was a great mum. Instead, I spent my time proving to Aurora that I was a super mum who's amazing at pretending she's an airplane!

We go about every day trying to show the world what great parents we are through social media. We show off what we buy them or how well they're doing because of us. What we should be doing is focusing on how our children see us, and not living up to everyone else's expectations.

Be present with your children, be mindful with them, because it won't be long before they don't want to play airplanes with us bare-footed.

Mindfulness teaches you that there are ways of communicating where you don't always have to be the person who sits nodding her head to the needs of others.

If you start small, like I did with the bedtime music, and then build up to putting your phone away more and focusing on things like tasting your food while you're eating it, you'll start to understand what mindfulness is all about. It can bring positivity and understanding into the present moment. In the past I ate so quickly that I was always the first one to finish, because I was so used to shoveling down my food to get to whatever I needed to do next. I now enjoy every bite and it's amazing.

The start of your mindfulness joinery won't be easy, but recognising that you need the change is the start of something powerful that will alter your whole approach.

I post a lot of mindfulness activities over on my Instagram blog @notjustamummy_world Have a look and see if you could use any of the activities as your first stepping stone.

Chapter Nine

The Active Mum

"I had to give up my dance classes when I had my twins. I never thought I would return but when they started school I had two days during the week that I could do the things I needed around them both and work commitments. I decided that on one of the days I would find a class close to me. Best thing I ever did because it was something I loved and that filled me up with energy and positivity that I now feed back into my family life." Caitlyn

As you modify your thoughts, it's important to do this for your body too, and be mindful that staying physically active does help.

When you're pregnant, it can feel like you can't do half the stuff you used to do. But many women have carried on with their usual activities, including exercise routines and felt amazing during pregnancy. Yes, they lowered it down to suit what they felt comfortable with and taking on board any medical guidance, but they never give up because it was one of the things they enjoyed doing, and a major part of their identity. They knew that if they didn't do it, they would feel lost, which I can one hundred percent relate to.

Never give up on something you love. Obviously, you have to risk assess physical activity and consult a professional, but it can be done. I didn't start new activities during pregnancy. I took long walks, as I always had, and that kept me sane and active.

But you might have to compromise in some areas. I made some big decisions during that third pregnancy. I decided to stop horse riding. Little did I know that I was going to make the decision to sell both of my horses soon after my daughter was born. But by then I knew that staying healthy and keeping my identity was about not trying to have everything. And this was healthier for everyone.

As good as I am at balancing and organising my life and my family's, I couldn't commit the time that both of the horses needed and deserved. As much as it hurt me to sell two important parts of my life that allowed me to feel carefree and empowered, I had made the right decision.

Shortly after letting go of something that you love, whether this is a hobby or a relationship, you can start to feel empty and useless. I didn't feel like that with this decision because, as we all know, caring for a baby is a full time role, so I was very content with knowing I did the right thing.

Along with mindfulness and physical activity leading to more rational decisions and thinking, I found writing a journal helped. Your mind is clouded from all of the bubbles building up from unwanted thoughts and feelings. Writing allows you to open up without the fear of rejection or disapproval. A journal can't tell you that you're being silly or that you will get over it; it simply soaks your words into its pages and allows you to pour out your deepest feelings and without any judgement. It won't make you feel like you're giving in or giving up. Because you're not.

Chapter Ten

You Don't Have to Change!

"I felt like I had to be a woman when I had my baby, but I still felt like a girl. I felt people didn't take me seriously because of the way I looked. A woman to me resembles power, strength, authority and I didn't feel any of them. My confidence went from 10 to 0 after I had my first child." Elizabeth

Change is inevitable. It's going to happen whether we're ready for it or not and there are a lot of changes during pregnancy and motherhood. I haven't got all the answers, not because I haven't experienced change, but because it affects everyone in different ways. But I think sharing my experiences can help you find your own path through change.

Creating a list of the changes that are happening, or have happened, will create a sense of being in control. You can start planning out the different options that will support you overcoming any negativity that change may bring along.

Changes that you might feel pressured into can include something as simple as clothing. But becoming a mum doesn't automatically mean that you swap the heels for the flats, (even though it is a lot easier to run after a toddler). No one is making you become someone you're not. So why do it? To fit in with the expected mummy style? To cover up more because you have a baby? You're now a mother so you mustn't do this or show that? Rubbish! Yes, you do change your mindset on clothing, and that is appropriate when you have a baby, but it's more about what is convenient. For instance, I didn't want to layer up when I was exclusively breastfeeding as it could be a nightmare with a hungry baby.

You can spend lots of time and energy worrying about your image. Even the thought of not having had your roots done in months can be stressful. This might be because of cost or energy levels, or maybe your baby won't settle with anybody else. You automatically think the worst, and sometimes even when you're only thinking about leaving your baby, he or she seems to already know what's going on. You will panic about how your baby will ever survive without you. You forget that other people share the same love, or have raised children themselves so know how to administrate a cup or a bottle of expressed or formula milk. But making the time for yourself will enhance what you have with your baby, not damage it or them.

Your energy levels aren't going to be the same if you're not looking after yourself. Aside from getting your hair done to feel better, this can even be as serious as the fuel you are putting into your body. Drinking lots of water does help me feel awake and clear headed. I never used to drink much water, but now I make sure I get as much as I can every day. It can be easy to forget when you're looking after a baby, but you need to keep yourself hydrated and healthy.
The last thing I want you not to change is a sense of what belongs to you.

Remember that a massive part of your identity are the things you own. It's not selfish to want to keep doing the things you enjoy and the objects that you deem as yours. I share things with my children, but there are things that I wouldn't want little hands to break and that's okay! It doesn't have to change.

Chapter Eleven

Mini Meltdown for Me

"I thought I had to tell all my family to come around to the house the day after coming home with my son. I didn't realise how tired I would be and straight away I regretted it as within the two hours that they were there I just wanted them to leave. I felt like I wasn't in control when realistically if I would have been honest about how I was feeling we could have re arranged. So why didn't I? I have no idea still to this day because my family only want the best for me and my son."
Katy

There would be times during my pregnancies, yes all three, where I could wake up after no sleep, or even a full night's sleep, and be in the worst moods. Moods that I thought only I understood. I was wrong of course. But God forbid anyone around me who second guessed why I was in these moods. I would snap at the smallest comment and the behaviour of those around me. Yes, I loved these people, but they drove me crazy when I was like this. It was even the way people ate or the smell of their perfume that got to me. The littlest of things would just send me into a complete craze of bitterness or tears.

I remember slowly lifting my head when we were all sitting around the table eating our family meal and all I could hear was food being chewed. It was like everyone had microphones strapped to their teeth. I had to ask them why they were all eating so loudly. As you can imagine there were a lot of shocked faces because they didn't realise they were. My senses were so heightened at that time. And of course they weren't doing anything out of the ordinary.

People talk about cravings during pregnancy, but for me it was these heightened senses, and this also included smells. Damp made me sick to my stomach. I had to smell my plates when they came out of the dishwasher because if they had been in there too long, they would smell noticeably different. At times I had to scrap food onto another plate, because that plate didn't smell normal to me. Sounds crazy doesn't it? You can only imagine what it looks like sniffing plates and cutlery in your kitchen.

Everything that wouldn't normally cause a trigger started to drown me in a state of confusion, tears and self-pity. I'm not usually one to expect the people around me to nurture my moods, but at those moments in my life I did. From the outside it looked like I wanted everything and everyone to disappear. Sometimes I did want to be on my own with my own feelings, tears and thoughts, but I also needed support.

It's like you want everyone to look after you but you can't stand anyone being close to you, touching you and trying to make you feel better about yourself. There were times when I knew I was to pushing away the people who were closest to me, through no fault of their own.

My husband and my little sister got the worst of my meltdowns. I remember a massive argument I had caused with my sister where she fired back a few home truths. This gave me a massive wake up call to how I had been talking to her. This wasn't me and even though we can look back now and move forward smiling, I do still appreciate the fact that they stood by me.

Speaking to other women and mothers from all walks of life, I realise that I'm not alone with feeling like this. Most women go through a rollercoaster of emotions during pregnancy, motherhood and life in general. I realised that the way I bottled it all up until I exploded didn't help me. Now I open up about even the littlest of things and I resolve them there and then. I don't let negative thoughts cost me my family and the people I love the most. I'm open, I'm honest and that's working for me and it can work for you too.

Chapter Twelve

Picture Perfect, well almost!

"Throughout my pregnancy I was adamant that I wasn't going to put any pressure on myself to breastfeed after reading how amazing it was, but how sometimes it doesn't always work out possible for mothers. I promised myself that I would let my daughter and my body decide. When my daughter was born she didn't latch on, so I decided to stick to my promise and I chose to formula feed. I had pressure from midwives and some friends telling me that I should have been breastfeeding, but I was happy with my decision. I had witnessed friends who had spent the first few weeks expressing, crying, trying desperately to get their babies to feed and genuinely believing that they were a failure if they couldn't breastfeed. Those same friends look back on their first few weeks of motherhood with sadness because of the pressure society put on them during pregnancy and those first stages of motherhood. Surely it should be what's best for mother and baby." Claire

As expected, my body changed during my pregnancies. I didn't put a lot of weight on, mainly due to the morning sickness, but I did gain a beautiful bump where my babies were developing. There were days when I would look down and smile knowing that my baby was safe and healthy. But then there would be times when I would feel irritable and huge and I would be counting down the days to my due date. It's a rollercoaster ride of so many thoughts and feeling.

Sometimes I would look down to admire my baby bump and my mind would tell me that my body was overweight and alien.

After I had my first baby, I was obsessed with losing weight and getting my body back in pre-pregnancy shape. I thought this was my own choice and it would make me feel so much better about myself. But it was insecurity about my relationship with my partner at the time. If only I'd confronted the truth then (that being a size eight doesn't keep people loyal), I might have enjoyed those first few weeks as a new mother a little bit better than I did.

I also had the picture-perfect images of the media and social media adding to this though, even without the influence of my partner at the time.

This was not my mind and body telling me to exercise or change my lifestyle, this was external pressure and it's not the healthy way of making changes. Making a change should be your choice.

We all have at least one friend on our social media whose life looks so beautiful and picture perfect, to the point where you think that they must have professional photographers. They never have a mental breakdown on their social media. You know those posts where you personally spend hours writing, delete every attempt, then finally get it right, post it and then immediately regret it.

Thinking that the time spent in that negative moment won't affect you or your life, isn't true. When you take a step back to see the bigger picture, it's you who has the problem here and not the person who has posted about their lives onto their own social media account. It hurts, I know! That moment when you're taking all of the rubbish, confusion, lack of sleep and craziness that is your own life, out onto people who don't even know you're doing it, and whose stories you don't know beyond social media.

That's not who you are, or what you believe in. Does driving negativity out onto our friends, family and complete strangers make our own lives more positive or make us feel any better inside? No, it doesn't. Reign this in and adapt a healthier approach to managing all of these unwanted and unneeded thoughts and behaviours.

Not feeling picture-perfect was one reason that I hibernated at the start of motherhood. The hibernation of a new mum is more common than I thought. I didn't realise that until I shared my story with other women who I trusted enough to know that they would not judge me or label me as a bad mother.

When I had my first baby, I wasn't aware of any baby classes or groups that I could go to and share my thoughts with other mums. There must have been local groups for me, we weren't in the stone ages as I'm only talking thirteen years ago, but I didn't know who to ask. I also didn't feel sure enough of myself as a mum to know that there are always ladies out there who will make you feel welcome.

The younger me thought all other mothers were glowing and happy with their lives. I didn't for one second feel like there was anyone in the world who could relate to what I was going through. Your mind does have a funny way of making you feel like you're alone, when in reality there are so many women who can connect with what you are experiencing.

I'm so grateful that I woke up to what was going on in my life. I realised that I had the power to overcome the obstacles that were causing me to slip into such a dark, lonely world. If you can't feel your own worth enough to make the changes needed, then reach out to the women around you. I guarantee it won't be long until you feel valued by yourself as you'll find that those women need your help too. Together you can support one another moving forward with your motherhood journeys.

Chapter Thirteen

Friendships

"My partner left not long after we had our first child together, and it hit me hard. I spent most of the time wondering how I would parent alone. It wasn't until my son's first birthday that I looked back at the year I had spent raising him alone that I realised I hadn't seen my friends unless it was a baby date." Melissa

During my pregnancy and early years of motherhood, I felt like I was losing friendships. There's a common belief that you find out who your true friends are during this time. But I have a different view on this now, which has saved many of my friendships.

Think about it this way; before you had children you had a different lifestyle, right? Okay, so you attracted certain friendships, and this is because of who you were and what your priorities were at the time. After having children, you know your life changes in so many ways, and this includes your priorities. You aren't always there for friends, which can cause people to drift apart. Some of your friends who haven't got children don't have to prioritise mummy life into their own. So, when you can't do a lunch or night out because of childcare, they will reach out to someone who can. Their lives don't have to stop for you.

Connecting with new mummy friends can support your wellbeing during this time. Meeting people at different stages in your life brings them in as a friend for a certain reason. I met a lot of friends when I was on maternity through the school playground and activities like baby massage classes.

My friendships with those before I had my third baby were still there; they had just taken a backseat to the baby activities and those who were on a similar life timetable to me. But I decided that I had to adjust my new life to my old friends too and not expect them to always change their routines for me. I was also prioritising myself when I made time to see my non-mum friends. I knew by letting them down that I would be letting myself down. So, I still made the effort to catch up even if it was just a cup of tea at my house. I found that they would regularly pitch in and help me get back on top of my life.

"That's what friends are for" came true for me.

I have a short activity that I think helps explain the shift in friendship dynamics and how you can adjust to this.
Think of yourself as a tree. Write everything about you on the trees bark; your name, when you were born, what colour eyes you have, your personality traits, basically everything that makes up you as a person.

Now move onto the roots. They represent your journey. You can write down what you think has kept you 'rooted' in your life before and after you had your child or children. This can be key friendships, family and big decisions you have made in life.

Let's look at branches. You need to add a new one for each momentous change in your life, another baby, a new job or a big life event like a marriage, anything that has shaped who you are today.

The leaves then represent your friends and family, everyone who surrounds you.

As time goes on, some leaves may fall off the tree, and that's okay. Life changes can be good, and not everyone who started your journey will continue on it. People have their own journeys and sometimes no matter how upsetting it may be, you have to focus on the positives and the other branches and leaves. A tree doesn't die if it loses a branch. It dies if the roots aren't firmly in the ground and being nourished by the water and food it needs to survive. My water and food now includes the self-love I have for myself, my mindfulness activities and the love from my family and friends.

But what can we do about the people who don't support us, the people who we have tried to reach out to, only to experience a negative reaction? I've got one bit of advice that will change your mindset towards these people. STOP! Yes, I said it, stop! Stop wasting your energy, time and breath on trying to create an acceptance with people like this. You're never going to change them or your own life while your energy is focused on making them want to help you or making them see things differently.

The motto to my motherhood is, ' My children and I are happy and healthy, and that's all that matters.'

If you chose to move forward without certain people, always make sure that you've done it for the right reasons. Be honest with yourself and with the people you've chosen to remove from your life. I choose the people who are in my life now. I live a happier, healthier life without the fear or reminder of negativity leaking into mine or my children's lives. This is a choice you have to make and a change that is needed.

Chapter Fourteen

Finding Myself

"When you are around people with negative energy, let it flow over you and not through you. It doesn't make you a bad person, or mean that you no longer want their friendship, it means you chose to take the energy you desire." Izabella Levey

Sitting at my dining room table after one of my first networking events as a new woman in business, I had this overwhelming feeling to sort my handbag out. Sounds crazy doesn't it, to think about your handbag after a business event?

Let me explain. During the event I had dipped into my bag for my business cards and noticed that it was full of my children's belongings. I had golf balls, unicorn lip balms, chocolate Christmas coins and much more. The only two things in there that were mine happened to be my purse (which might as well have been the children's too) and my passport. I looked in it to see my own picture staring back at me with my name, Clare Bowers, sitting beside it. Yes, that was me and this was MY bag. In that moment I realised that wanting it back wasn't such a crazy thought. This might seem like a small step, but it was part of switching my focus back to my own identity.

For the next few months I could reach into my handbag and pull my things out, objects that belonged solely to me and it made me feel great! Try it for yourself and see how you feel. I would love to hear what results you get from this first step. From clearing my bag, I went to clearing my head of all of the to do's I had over the next few months for the children. I found a diary just for their activities which helped me to keep everyone organised. I switched to asking some new questions like, what day I can meet friends for lunch and could I schedule in some business calls. It felt good. I enjoyed putting myself on the front line of priority alongside my children.

Starting with the little things that only you would notice, like a good clear out of your handbag, is a positive start that will set you on the path to bringing yourself back as the main character in your life.

Chapter Fifteen

Extending the family

"I didn't spend long enough getting to know my ex-partner before I moved him in with my children. The pressure of three children put a new strain on us and we ended up separating within a few months. I do believe that I rushed things because I felt so happy and I wanted to share that happiness with my children. I'm grateful that they were only young and don't remember this relationship because it consisted of a lot of arguments in a stage that was meant to be full of excitement and learning about one another." Sandra

It's hard to think about a new relationship or extending your family when you already have children. I was also worried about what everyone else would think about me wanting that little bit more for myself.

I attempted to have a relationship with a childhood friend when my older children were toddlers, but it didn't work out because I thought I didn't have the time to commit. I made up that excuse because I didn't want anyone to judge me going into a new relationship when they were so young. I assumed that's how the people around me would see it. Looking back, I realise that those same people I was worrying about would have been supportive. Fear held me back from putting my own needs first.

Years flew by and my children were growing up quickly and becoming more independent. I started to feel like I wasn't needed as much, and they preferred playing with their friends than me. It took me a while to get used to the fact I wasn't in demand. I found myself having the time to buy books and actually get to read them without any distractions. It was lovely, but I knew there was something missing.

This is where social media played a massive part in my happiness. I posted a picture of my car failing to get me from A to B again and my phone quickly beeped. I checked the notification and it was the childhood friend, the one I had tried to have a relationship with all those years ago.

The comment was asking if I needed any help because he had a garage in the area. I replied that I did, and like a knight on a horse he came to the rescue and fixed the car. I offered to buy him lunch one day in-between my working hours as a thank you. He agreed, and we met a few more times as friends. But that didn't last long when we realised that there was still something between us.

Telling people about my new relationship was daunting. I would start it with, 'You know Alan, don't you? Well ...' I don't know why I was so nervous because my family already knew and loved him. I think it was because I still had the cloud hanging over me from when I ended the relationship all those years before, questioning if I was truly ready for a relationship and how I was going to introduce him to my children as a boyfriend. Would they all get on or was I heading into battle?

So how long is the acceptable amount of time to wait before you introduce someone new to your children? I personally don't think there is a set time. It varies from family to family depending on the ages of the children and whether you want that little bit longer in the new relationship stages with only you as a priority.

Understanding that you can have a relationship, without having to share anything with your children and family at first, can give you more time to get to know one another. This is without any distractions like the opinions others may have. It also gives you the chance to understand how you feel and if it's serious enough to then introduce your new partner and welcome him into the family.

I can safely say that I enjoyed this time of being Clare. I didn't have to look after Alan like I did my children. He was taking care of me, treating me with flowers and taking me for lunch. This was something that I wasn't used to and admittedly it felt good to have the roles reversed. Walking out of my front door was like something out of a Superman film, where he changes quickly from Clark Kent to Superman. I felt like I had transformed from Mum to Clare.

I had no yogurt in my hair and not a care in the world because I knew my children were safe and that I was allowed to go out and have time with Alan on our own.

It got to the stage in the relationship where it felt right for the children to meet Alan. I introduced him as a friend and we enjoyed days out to the cinema and walks in the park, so my children could get to know him before we moved to the next stage of telling them that we were boyfriend and girlfriend. This sounds so childish but that's what it was.

I didn't have to wait long until my son was asking for Alan to stay over with us. He enjoyed listening to all of Alan's stories about being in the military, because to him they were a lot more interesting than my own Royal Navy tales. They both got on so well.

I asked my daughter how she felt about Alan moving in and she said, 'It's good because you are happier and so are we.' This was lovely to hear, even though I didn't want her thinking I wasn't happy being a mum, because I truly was. I was just missing one of the puzzle pieces that made our life what it is now, which feels whole, and that was Alan.

My children adapted very well to Alan moving in. They understood that change doesn't have to be negative, even though past experiences had been, including moving homes and their dad leaving. Now we had exciting opportunities, including another new home and a new addition to the family with a baby sister for them.

You never know what saying yes to an opportunity will bring. This relationship taught me that holding back because of fear only results in chances passing you by and I was not letting Alan pass me by again. Have the courage to speak out about the things you want and make an emotional commitment to holding onto them. This is not because it keeps everyone happy or content, but because it makes you happy and creates your own chapters.

Introducing a new partner to your children isn't always going to be a smooth journey. We still have the ups and our downs in our home that come with all family life. But I know starting a new chapter with Alan was the best decision I could have made for myself and my children. I feel a love like no other and my children have another person in their lives who would do anything in his power to keep them protected.

Getting married was the next stage for us and it was something I never thought would happen to me. When I was a single mum, I had been living in the money mindset that it came in and went out again straight away, because that's always what seemed to happen. So, when Alan asked me to marry him it was one of those moments where I was taken aback. I didn't hesitate when saying "yes" but I automatically wondered how we were going to afford a wedding. But we managed it and it was the most magical day of our lives next to having our children.

I was overwhelmed with happiness, even though a few comments were made that it was too soon, only being a few months into the relationship. But for anyone who knew me, Alan and the children, their reply would have been that it was a bit late and that we should have done it years ago! I didn't care what anyone else thought or said though, what mattered was my little family were all happy and safe.

You can't please everyone. Reminding yourself that you are a priority and drowning out any negativity is a must do to make sure you don't let any flow into your family unit and affect your relationship.

Worrying about moving forward with a relationship because of your ex-partner and children's father doesn't mean that it shouldn't happen either. Keeping communication open but not forcefully will help things flow. You are no longer a couple, but you are still parents who are setting examples for your children.

Chapter Sixteen

What will they think?

"When I first brought my adopted son home, I went for it with local 'mother and baby' groups just to get us out of the house. I tried so hard to talk to other mums and make friends, but I struggled. I didn't have a partner to talk about. I hadn't given birth to him or been through labour; I hadn't had the opportunity to breastfeed. This is the kind of support that 'regular' mums need and I'm not knocking that, I just felt like I had nothing in common with them.

"I joined online groups too and remember commenting on a post about teething. My son's foster carers used an amber teething anklet and I continued with this and I swear it worked. So, I recommended this, not realising how controversial this subject was! Things like this knocked my confidence. I thought I was helping my baby, yet there were people telling me that it was wrong, posting links about children dying after choking on them, and all kinds of scientific research telling me how rubbish they were.

"My little boy is 2 now and I look back and get annoyed about how hard I tried to please others. We can all be cruel and judgmental towards each other but most of all we can be cruel to ourselves. None of us are perfect, we do things our own way, we're mostly winging it and we all make mistakes. Now that I'm feeling confident as a mum the only advice I give to others is to only ever judge yourself by looking at your children. If they are healthy and happy, well mostly happy (or as happy as a 2-year-old who knows his own mind can be!!), then you are doing a grand job." Jennie

Whether it is losing weight, changing your hair colour, or buying a new car, most people will have an opinion on it. They will want to know why you changed and they will tell you what they think of this and what they predict is going to happen next. This is natural and out of your control. However, how you choose to react to it, is in your control. I like the phrase, 'stop, think, then react.' But I'm human too, so this doesn't always go to plan!

Sometimes what other people think won't sit with your own morals. For me it hit home when I was put off breastfeeding because I was told it was very time consuming and I had two older children to think about. I understand that breastfeeding can be difficult for some mothers, but I would never judge or question another woman on how she was preparing to feed her baby.

It's healthy to want the people who surround your children to be on the same moral wavelength as you. It doesn't mean that you think you are above or below the people in your life. It just means that your priorities as a parent have influenced your decisions.

This is a vital part of building on your identity, as you are seeing things from a different view, a mother's view. Go with your heart and don't worry about what everyone else will think. You know what's best for you and your family. This is the healthier option than the alternative, where you allow yourself to drown in other people's morals, living their beliefs and being untrue to your own.

Social media can be a key area. I have mentioned before that you need to use it in the right way and find the right communities. The ones that I am involved in now add positivity, encouragement and balance to my life. These ladies make me feel like me again. We have conversations about us as women and also about our family life. It's important to surround yourself with like-minded people who you can turn to for support on a 'not so good but I don't want to talk about it' day.

Joining a pregnancy group in your area, or online can be rewarding, but can also have its downside. It's too easy to get swept into conversations regarding birth, health and education. Although anecdotal advice can be very useful, you should still consult your community or hospital midwife with any worries or problems that may be causing you concern.

I've been given advice around sleep routine for the last three years for my youngest child and most of it I found very rewarding but the rest, well it didn't suit my situation. I mean how can I put my daughter to bed every night at 7pm when some days my son attends football sessions until 8pm? It's okay giving out and taking advice but please remember everyone's situations are different and what works for you won't necessary work for everyone else.

It's so easy to think that you are taking up your midwife's time by sending her a quick message or booking in an extra appointment. But your midwife is there for your wellbeing just as much as they are there for your baby's. Talk to them openly about how you are feeling. There is nothing embarrassing that you can say that I'm sure they haven't already heard before.

One conversation with a friend, family member or professional can make a massive difference to those first few years of motherhood.

But one of the many questions that repeatedly crosses my mind is, do we act differently around other mothers to get their approval? My answer ten years ago would have been yes, but now I've broken free of this mindset. I almost lost my identity trying to be like other mums. I can now say that I don't try to be anyone else. I'm happy with who I am, and I would never want to change anything about myself, especially to please others.

Chapter Seventeen

Losing control

"I was adamant that I didn't want any drugs during my birth. I wanted to keep it as natural as possible, but it didn't turn out the way I had planned. During my labour, it was in my best interest and my baby's, to be taken down to theatre and have a c-section. I was upset but I knew I had no other choice. It was an experience that I had to repeat to nearly everyone who met me and my newborn. I kept replaying the fact that it didn't go the way I wanted. For months I would say that I didn't get to do it the way that I wanted to but then looking back now it actually did go the way I wanted to. I gave birth to my healthy baby and I made that decision to trust the professional. Even though at the time it didn't feel like I was in control, I actually was. I was just being guided to change the course slightly, but the outcome was exactly what I had wanted. Sometimes it might not feel like we are in control but clearing your mind and seeing the positive in everything you do, does open your mind to understanding your own control." Kayleigh

It's pretty hard not to try and keep up with those around you and their expectations. This doesn't mean that you are losing the race, because life isn't a race, it's a journey. But if someone says you need to be visiting family with your newborn, getting back into your routine or fitting into those skinny jeans, you automatically believe that's what you should be doing, and you question why you're not already there.

The problem lies with the fact that other people don't know how ready you are for any of this, because they aren't recovering from having just given birth. Their minds are replaying their own experiences, so will naturally assume that you can do what they could do in the same time period. And of course people can forget how hard it was. Everyone is different, and they don't know how you're feeling on the inside, as both your mind and your body are healing from something so physically draining. For me there was nothing worse than someone telling you how quickly they were back driving or to their pre-pregnancy size.

Whether you're a new mother, or a mother of two, three or more children it can feel like you're losing control over every little thing, from choices during pregnancy and birth to being home and starting your parenting journey. This is especially if you had a tough time during childbirth and are in need of that extra bit of support.

But too many people crowding you in your home can become seriously overwhelming. So, how do you create that balance to keep you and everyone else happy? Hang fire! See how I automatically asked how to keep everyone else happy? This is a common slip and the opposite of what you should do. I cared about my family and friends' wellbeing during this time of course, but realistically I was the one who had gone through three days of labour, lost a large amount of blood and was physically drained. But how could they know how I was feeling if there wasn't any communication from me? Staying in control means you must share how you're feeling and say what you want. My husband's favourite phrase when I was pregnant was, 'Well, how was I to know? I'm not a mind reader.' How true are his words!

You don't have to think about anybody else at this stage. Some mothers might feel like they can get back up and take over the world, but it doesn't have to be that quick.

Taking time out for yourself is what is needed for those first few days. I know how hard that can be, especially if you have older children who depend on you, or your partner has to return to work. Even the simple things can get to you, like washing piling up and the dishwasher not being turned on for days. So, how do you cope with this?

DELEGATE! Delegating can be hard work at the best of times, but when you're pregnant or you've just had your baby, it can seem impossible. No one does it like you, right? So, what's the point because you have to go over it anyway? There's a big point. It will give you time on your own and to bond with your new baby, without having to multitask. It's the time to sit back and allow motherhood to catch up, and to let the realisation of the changes that are happening to your body and mind settle. It's the time to pick up that book you didn't finish, while your new baby is feeding.

The importance that surrounds a new mum bringing her baby home, is sometimes forgotten about. The amount of times I've heard new mums say that they would have preferred to come home, settle in and then see visitors, is increasing. It's only right that everyone wants to meet the new addition, but this can be worked around the needs of the mum.

When you become a mother, it can feel like you have to learn quickly and relate to what motherhood is all about, opening up a whole new perspective on life and the challenges it brings.

I believe that all visitors' attention should be focused and directed at both mother and baby. Questions like, 'do you want a cup of tea?' or 'do you want to go and lie down or for a walk by yourself?' can make a massive difference to how a mum is feeling and open up the communication doors to see if there is anything troubling her.

I'm sure you can relate to a time when you've gone past the stage of reasonable thinking. It's like a switch just seems to click in your mind. Everything goes dark and it feels like you have blanked out. Then you suddenly come back into reality, and no one even noticed that you weren't there for moment.

That's one of the loneliest things you can experience as a mother. It feels as if no one cares, but realistically how can anyone notice if you're not prepared to talk about what's going on?

Communicate, Delegate and Concentrate on yourself. The positives will then flow.

Chapter Eighteen

Look at Me

"Sometimes I felt it was better to just be quiet and get on with it because I didn't want to sound silly or as if I didn't know what I was doing." Claire

Fears from past experiences, like being told you're doing something wrong, not feeling like you've got anyone who understands you or a relationship ending, can hold us back from reaching our life goals. Whether that's building your own empire or even just getting out of the house for a walk, sometimes we find it hard to admit that the past is restricting us from moving forward.

Set a clear vision of what it is that you want to talk about and write down notes if it helps you. Open up and speak out. Make it clear as day when you are asking for support. Even if you don't have all of the answers, start small and tell those close to you that have a problem that you need help with. Holding everything inside just makes it harder to release when it gets too much. I personally know how messy it can get when you've kept everything in for so long that you explode with emotions.

A perfect example that was explained to me during a workshop I attended in a school, was to imagine the children's emotions being the bubbles in a bottle of pop. The child might shake them in the morning before school from negative words, actions and behaviour of those who surround him or her. And we all know what happens when you disturb a bottle of pop. So, when the child came to school, our approach was to open that lid of emotions gently and mindfully, so that the bubbles, aka emotions. didn't spill out all over the place, but instead released the pressure slowly, causing minimal mess and distress.

This theory fits in perfectly with some of the stories I've heard across my platform of women, many who build up so much emotion through pregnancy and motherhood that it all gets too much, and they explode. This is why we need to feel comfortable with speaking out and supporting one another though the tough times as well as the happier times.

You can keep so much to yourself that the negative thoughts and emotions start to become your natural way of thinking. They overrun your rational thoughts and drown any positivity out of you. It then becomes easier to give in to them.

Those negative thoughts start to leak through your words, your actions and your behaviour. You can become unrecognisable to everyone around you, and most importantly, to yourself.

Who is this woman? Why am I shouting so much? Why am I crying all the time? And why do I spend my days talking to myself in my head about my worries and not to those who love and support me?

This isn't like you, you know this. What does help is to focus on the present moment and reach out to those around you.

Chapter Nineteen

Relationships

"Sometimes it might be easier to think of myself as single because that's how it feels for me when I talk to my partner. I don't get any of his affection or his time anymore. I know it shouldn't feel like this, but I am lonely." Emily

It's hard to know where to start when it comes to talking about the relationships worries and challenges that we can face during pregnancy and motherhood. It can be a rollercoaster of a ride that can make you and your partner feel like you would rather get off at times, than enjoy and embrace the experience.

People often look like they have the perfect relationship. But I compare this to reading a book in a busy environment when you only skim it and get half the reality. If you were to sit down with the book and take the time to focus, you would see it properly. This is just as you would know the relationship reality of couples with or without children, if you spent more time with them.

When I first became a mother, I found it hard to make time for anything else. Every second seemed to be taken up by a to-do list for my baby. I forgot to nurture the relationship with my partner. I can relate to mothers who feel like they lose all time and energy for their partners without even realising it is happening. Before having children, I can imagine you were both used to leaving the house when you wanted, to visit the cinema or to go shopping and for a bite to eat, and bedtime would be your own time and space.

The truth is that nobody wants a relationship to go off track and become something that you don't enjoy or feel passionate about. Losing someone from your life hurts no matter how tough we appear to be. There is something deep about a separation that can make you question your whole life.

But if your partner loves you, that love carries on through the difficult times. Yes, having a baby affects your relationship, of course it does. You've both got this new responsibility, this tiny little life who depends on you for everything.

The dynamics of a relationship can change massively. This doesn't have to be in a negative way. After all, having a child is a sign of how much you love one another and the start of your family life together. But the whole relationship can steer itself to focus solely on your baby's needs forgetting about the needs that your relationship requires to nurture it and keep it healthy and content.

My solution would be to try and make time together to do things that you both enjoy which remind you just how much you both love each other. If you're anything like me and my husband, you'll spend the first hour talking about how you think the kids are getting on at home! But try to switch off and appreciate the time together, and yes that means putting those phones aside.

In the past I know my husband has called during the day and my mind has been somewhere else, thinking about the things that need doing or an upset with the children. I would try to contribute to the conversation, but the challenges of getting the kids ready, doing the tea or answering that email back, would outweigh his voice. I would end up asking him repeated questions, trying my best to show him I was listening. It's tough having a partner who works away and who can't take over the bedtime routine, homework or one to one time with the children while you have that long soak in the bath you've been dreaming about all day.

So, how can you make the 'Mummy-Time' and 'Me-Time' I've previously mentioned and 'Husband/Boyfriend/Partner-Time' work? How can you fit it all in? My main tip would be to communicate and plan. I know this isn't easy when you have such a busy lifestyle and a new baby, but writing in a family calendar that everyone can see can help you to keep one step ahead.

You could also try and write down all of your vulnerabilities and concerns as a couple. This may include sleep deprivation, money worries, the children's development or just thinking that one of you is doing more than the other. Seeing it in black and white can make you both realise how you can support each other and enjoy your parenthood and relationship at the same time.

Chapter Twenty

Work Life for Mum

"Time off again for your daughter's appointments? Yes, I was actually asked that even though my employer knew I didn't have any support when it came to splitting appointments because I had moved away from my family and friends for my new promotion earlier on that year. It got that bad that I stepped down from the position and moved back home for family support. I couldn't decide if it was because I couldn't keep up with the work load because I found my new position a lot harder or the pressure coming from being a single mother even though my daughter was in senior school and was pretty independent. I'm now working for a new company in an even higher position but this time I'm closer to my family and friends and it has made a massive difference having a company that understands I might have to take time off for appointments, but having that understanding there for my employer meant I didn't mind also staying longer when they needed me to." Carly

Going back to work is a worry that is sure to cross every mother's mind. You have so many questions: Should I change my hours? What happens if my baby is sick? Will work understand? You want to have all this answered before you make any life-changing decisions, but you're also so busy right up until you go back, that you push all this to one side.

I didn't want to return to work after my third baby, but I needed to assess the financial reality of this. It was a decision that took time. However, I did make a few impulsive decisions like taking my children out of kids' club even though I knew there was a waiting list to go back in! I was thinking about how we could save money there and then over the difficulty of getting them back in if I returned to work.

Feelings about going back to work will vary from woman to woman. I understand that completely. How you're feeling will depend on your personality, job role, your employer, your own baby's needs and the financial needs of your household.

My work ethos before having children was very different to what it was after I had my first child, second child and now my third child. It changed with the life lessons I learned and experiences that shook me.

I was once asked by an employee if I had anyone else to pick my son up after I received a call from the school telling me he wasn't well and had to come home. I didn't want anyone else looking after my son and, more importantly, I wanted to take him to the doctors and home to rest myself. I learned that not all employers understand this.

Your employer may pay you during time off for family matters but, in some cases, they don't have to. This is why it's a must for everyone to check their contract, company handbook or intranet site to see if there are rules about this. Each workplace will vary.

This can be a worry for working mothers, because we all know children being sick can come without any warning. When my older children were little I would quote to them a line that my mother would say to me before school if I didn't feel well- that if I was very sick then my teacher would call her and send me home. Looking back, I know that my mum didn't say it because she didn't want to look after me at home, but because she had work commitments.

Before having my children, I had the mindset that making money meant that I had to work long hours for a boss. For a few years I truthfully enjoyed getting up, getting ready, getting through the working day and then doing as I pleased, and then doing it all again. I also had very few financial worries. Back then I didn't have to worry about anything major other than feeding myself and my train journey home.

As you can probably imagine when I had my first child I found it more difficult to work full time around his needs, and then a year later my daughter's needs. Two children a year apart both experiencing teething, temperatures and often not sleeping all night took its toll on my energy levels and commitment to work.

Returning to work was one of the biggest challenges I had to overcome but I managed to secure a job in customer service. I realise now it was the pressure to return to work that made me accept the interview that led to the job. My children went to a private nursery and I carried out the same routine for a lot longer than I wanted to. It consisted of a quick walk to nursery pushing a double pram, kissing my children goodbye and then running, and I mean running, to the train station to travel thirty minutes to a job I didn't enjoy. I would then finish, jump on the train, collect my children, return home, cook supper and then fall asleep with them.

I didn't make any friends at that job. I felt like I didn't have the time. It upsets me even to this day thinking about how unapproachable I must have appeared. But I was afraid of letting people in and letting people down.

Eventually, I made the decision to change my career to one I thought I would be happier in. I got a job supporting children in schools. It fitted in with my own motherhood plan perfectly, being term-time only. I didn't have to depend on childcare when they were off school, which I was truly grateful for, as there are a lot of mothers who wouldn't have this option. The pay wasn't great for the energy that went into every day, but the children I worked with made it rewarding.

However, during my time off, I felt like I had to spend every waking hour with my own children, because they didn't have both parents at home. And I was still in the get up, go to work, come home, eat, sleep and repeat pattern. So, I knew that eventually something would have to change with this too.
If you are in the position where you can take support from family, this can release so many of the built-up anxieties that come with the return to work. Can anyone look after the baby for you so that childcare costs are reduced, and you can return to work part-time or maybe spend some hours building up your own business?

After having my third child, I decided not to go back to the school I worked in. I was lucky that this was a financially viable option. Okay, it wasn't a situation that was bringing loads of money to the table, but it did take away the nursery and childcare bills. If I'm honest this probably would have been around the same amount as my wage. Shocking I know. This is why I understand when mothers tell me that they can't afford to go back to work. You can literally be covering just your outgoings!

But as the months went by, I began to miss the children and the staff. They had been a massive part of my journey. I would also start to miss having a career that gave me an identity beyond being a mum.

I would hear more and more success stories from women who were running their own business around family life. But at the time I thought that I couldn't do it. I soon proved myself wrong.

One lady who inspired me raised three children alone and runs a very successful business. Even she admitted she wished she had a second pair of hands. I related massively with her because I also have days when I wish there were another four of me. But she still made it work. I knew that I could too.

Chapter Twenty One

A School Run Mum

"You can't treat motherhood with the same schedule you would use in a 9-5 job." Louise

In some workplaces you're going to be surrounded by people who aren't very supportive or understanding when it comes to time off for family matters. Once again, their opinion or attitude is out of your control; it should not affect the choices you make. There are rights to protect working mothers and allow for flexibility.

I spent so much time in work when my two older children were growing up that I didn't meet teachers until I could make parents evening. When I married my husband and fell pregnant I was given my maternity leave early because of my sickness. This gave me a chance to catch up on everything I had missed out on. I loved being a school run mum. I'm serious, I was so excited to meet other mums and be there to hear all about my children's day as they raced out of the school doors towards me.

For the first few weeks I was always on time, both morning and after school, until the reality of not having to be anywhere other than home hit and my children began to relax too much. They knew that if they forgot their PE kit, I would shoot down the school to drop it off. I thought being a working mum with a strict routine was the dark side. This was before I had this experience of being a stay at home mum, which for me was just as tough and sometimes even tougher!

Being a stay at home mum on maternity leave before I had my third baby, I would spend a lot of time thinking about what was happening in work. Did the staff and children miss me? Had someone else taken my role over? Were they better than me? I had to learn how to switch work life off from home life, which isn't easy, but speaking to and spending more time with friends and family members who didn't mind me not being very energetic was a massive help.

I also started to notice the other working mums at the school dropping their children off. I wondered how they were doing it so gracefully and, more to the point, how did they work their hours around the school run? I began to make friends with some of the mums and I learnt that by communicating with their employer about hours and family commitments they felt reassured that their employers understood. This wasn't the case for everyone though.

When my children were in nursery, I went to work wondering how they were getting on and if they were missing me. I'm sure all mothers think like that when returning to work. I still miss all three of my children during the day and when they aren't around me. But I know they're fine and I make an effort to be fully in the present moment when I'm with them.
I do believe that mums suffer a terrible amount of natural separation anxiety. No matter how many times I wanted to believe that it was my baby who missed me and who wouldn't settle with anyone else, it was often me building this up. The last thing I wanted to hear was, 'She will be okay.' Even though I knew she would be, my mind didn't allow me to think that.

If you're spending hours at work thinking about how your baby is getting on in nursery give them a call on your break or ask them to send updates. This will bring a lot of reassurance.

I still worry when my children are out of my sight, but it also doesn't stop me from working hard for my business to provide for their futures. It's getting that happy medium when it comes to taking control of your thoughts and putting them into perspective. You know your own personal reasons for getting up and going out to work. You must also remind yourself that if it's not making you happy or giving you the outcome needed, then think outside the box and come up with a plan of change. I'm not suggesting that all mothers want to change their jobs, because they don't, but you deserve to be happy. There will always be an answer to the barriers.

Chapter Twenty Two

Routine and Focus

"I would dread anyone asking me to do anything past 7pm, not because I disliked the people who were asking, but more because I didn't have any energy to get excited. Sounds lazy but I had recently given birth to twins and they had control over my every move, with how their night and day had gone." Vivienne

So, how did I become more focused and what did I do about my routine? One thing I did was to stop looking at the time. This helped my work flow and progress. When I wasn't clock-watching to see if it was nearly home time, the day went a lot faster.

I switched from a mum who was worrying about her children, thinking about the ten million things that she had to do when she got home, to living my work day in the present moment. I took longer to read over emails, and although I couldn't always book clients in around the children, I came to an agreement with myself. If it wasn't realistically possible then I wasn't allowed to beat myself up about it. It took a while to get used to this, especially when I added in putting my phone away. I knew my children's school had my home phone number and would call through if anything was wrong. Firing through emails without any stop start process, I was getting more done in a shorter time frame.

I also created a new routine for my children. It would start with my favourite three Bs, which are Bath, Book and Bed. I spent so much time repeating myself, shouting from one end of the house to the other, before I established this. My children all learnt that once I had announced that the Bs were starting, that this mum meant business! Everyone, including me, had to switch off from the outside world, stop watching TVs and iPads and put away phones. It resulted in us all getting a better night's sleep. Although my toddler does still manage to end up co-sleeping at some point in the night and I'm still working on the ownership of my bed!

My individual part of the daily routine would be to wake up before any of the others, have a nice cup of tea and double check my to do list of the day. My phone stays downstairs as I wake all three children up, then we get ready and they go to school and nursery. I found that I would be ready and charged up for a day of work and everything ran more smoothly. However, there will always be some bumps in the road.

My toddler had a spell where she would wake up three to four times a night and I would be physically and mentally drained from the lack of sleep. When this would happen when I worked in the school, I would have no other choice than to get up and power through it on an overload of coffee. But now I reflect and ask myself how I can help my body and mind gain more energy through my food and by getting extra rest.

I'm sure you all know this isn't as easy as it sounds but ask your partner or family member to take over the reins as you recharge.

If you're thinking that it would make things a lot easier if you did have your own business that worked around your children and family commitments, then start by thinking about something that you love and enjoy doing. Whatever it is, write it down and envision ideas on how this can generate an income. The love of sewing could result in having your own classes, for example. You never know until you mind map and dive into it. Your business idea should come in the form of something that you're passionate about.

Whether you choose to set up your own business, or return to work, how can you overcome the initial fear of 'what if'? I would suggest focusing on the identity benefits. You have an opportunity to be 'you' away from your mum role and to create money while doing this.

I'm talking mums having a career and enjoying it. Working can make you feel alive, empowered and it can be an escape from running around juggling the children and the house. Yes, sometimes work is a break from the reality of motherhood, is that so wrong to admit? Not at all.

If you're due to return to work listen to what it is that you truly want and then realistically plan the outcome that you would like. You might just be a little bit nervous to return because you've been off and don't know if things have changed, or you might seriously want a change yourself and becoming a mother opened your mind to that.

I learnt a valuable lesson during my maternity leave too - that whenever I went back to work, I would not let work life cloud my personal life. I was finally awake to how other mums managed their jobs around their children and it looked great!

Chapter Twenty Three

Money, Money, Money

"The most difficult times were when I had more money going out than coming in. I would have to budget and not allow biscuits and treats in the shopping basket. I would sometimes miss payments on school lunches and hope the other kids in their classes wouldn't notice that brown slip to remind their mum that she hadn't paid on time." Alicia

One day the reality of being a single mum came crashing down on me like a ton of bricks. At the time I thought my little world was going to collapse. I received a message during my lunch hour from my landlord. He needed to move back into his house.

Upset and confusion raced through my mind. I could rent another house, but I had my routine in place and didn't have the mental space for a change like this at that moment. This was also a point in my life when I didn't have any spare cash.

What if I couldn't find anywhere else within my budget? The children were settled and loved the house and area we lived in. The mum guilt overload kicked in massively. Instead of owning up to the fact that I needed help, and being desperate to keep up the image of being a self-sufficient single mum, I went back into the staffroom as though everything was okay. I would return home and sob uncontrollably into my pillow, thinking that I was the world's worst mother. I eventually reached out to my close friend Michele who supported me with house viewings. This was even though I had let her down so many times and had cancelled plans with her since becoming a mum. We found a perfect house that I could afford, which was in fact closer to my children's school.

While all this was going on in my crazy world, my children didn't know just how hard their mum was beating herself up about how rubbish she thought she was making their lives. I worked, but I still couldn't afford to buy them the expensive presents that other children their age had or take them on holidays. I was lucky that they didn't even notice what everyone else had and they were grateful for even the smallest of gifts.

No matter how hard I worked or budgeted, sometimes I would have no other option than to ask family for financial support. Those were the times I felt like a failure. But in the end, it brought us closer together as they wanted to, and could, help me. And they knew that I would have done the same for them.

For women who earn as much, or more than their partners, the financial strain of running a household falls on both the mother and the father. But women lose pay on maternity leave. For instance, from nine months in, the government doesn't provide any statutory pay at all and most employers have long stopped their maternity pay schemes.

Back then I didn't realise the amount of other working mothers, single or with partners, who were experiencing the same struggles as I was. We all hide it well when we don't want others to see any problems with our lives. This is sad when it gets to the point of living a lie both in work and at home.

There is no need to do this. Work and home life can be made so much easier by reaching out, listening to and supporting each other where possible.

Chapter Twenty Four

I Can't Do Everything!

"I went back to work when my daughter was 6 months old because we couldn't survive on another cut to my maternity pay. My daily routine turned into autopilot. I was awake most of the night with my daughter. I struggled getting up and giving 100% to my work commitments, driving home, picking my daughter up and then returning home to be mum and wife for the rest of the evening. I was physically drained but didn't see a way out of it because this was my life now. I turned to my friend who was also a working mum and she gave me tips like buying a slow cooker and jumping the train to work instead of driving to tackle emails before I got home. That supported me in having some quality time with my husband and myself."Chelsy

Imagine standing in the middle of a room with all your family, friends, children, employers, clients, health professionals and social media surrounding you. It already sounds uncomfortable to me! Now imagine the sound and the vibrations there would be if everyone in the room started to shout your name, craving your attention. You want to please everyone, because you don't want them to feel as if their voices are not important.

This can happen without everyone being in the room with you; even when sitting at home on your couch alone. Repeated demands stick in our minds. Who needs me and who shall I prioritise? I know, let me see how far I can stretch myself across everyone's needs except, of course, my own.

Does this sound like something that you can relate to? It's like you're getting pulled from pillar to post, person to person and you're just expected to go with it, or so you have trained your mind to believe. Your attention is in demand, and you've never been so popular for fixing the everyday challenges that everyone around you are facing and coming to you for support with.

There are times when my husband was working away that I would spend over two hours getting my toddler into her bedtime routine. I'd then come out of her room to be greeted with the needs of my older children. Sometimes it would be help with homework or to share something that they were excited about.

This can be the time when you feel like dropping everything around you, going to your room and climbing back under those covers, right? I feel your frustration. No matter how much you get done, nothing ever seems to stay the away you intended it to. The washing piles up and the kids want three different meals. You get to the stage where something has to give. Your body can't go on being in such demand, and your mind doesn't know what day it is.

Having been told in the past that this was just life, and that it's your own fault for having children, doesn't help. Ignore anyone who says that. If anything, it makes you feel as though there is nothing that needs changing, because it's life, right? Wrong! Your life doesn't have to make you feel so low and so powerless to change. This force of negativity that is thrown at you, can be the energy and determination that you need to push things forward and make the changes.
No one should ever make you feel like you are fighting a losing battle, especially those who you are close to. This is your battle and you are the only one who can take back the reigns , canter through the mess and come out the other side.

Only you can decide what path you want to ride down. So why do we let the beliefs, views and negativity of others determine what our next step is, or what our life goals are? Why are we so reluctant to take back control and show the people around us that we can get through this? Because we keep telling ourselves that we can't, but the sooner you start to tell yourself that you can, then things will change.

Now you can see that no-one can do everything, and appearances are deceptive, the next step is to focus on your health.

A lot of built up pressure and stress can come from trying to get too much done in an unrealistic time.

Managing the needs and demands of your new baby and combining everything into a routine for you and your family can be challenging on its own, without the pressure of everyday tasks and to dos hanging over like a grey cloud. A cloud that when ignored grows bigger and bigger until we realise that it's an area that needs some attention.

Even before I became a mother I would feel like I was always expected to do everything because I had no family commitments. This was seen as free time to some of the people I worked with, especially during times like Christmas holidays.

When I left the Royal Navy to have my son, I thought people would tell me that I was silly giving up an excellent career to start a family when in fact, no one blamed me for anything. I had so much support from friends and family but I just didn't stop to notice it when I was too busy worrying.

Women in business often ask how I manage to juggle work commitments, family and friends. It's about focus and being in the moment, knowing what needs to be done as a priority and what can wait. Sometimes I carry over my to do list into the next day because I know realistically I won't get them done.

For me, if I know I've got parents evening on Tuesday I make that evening all about that. It's simple; nothing else will be booked in. If I'm out with the children for the day, I focus on them and their needs, then I timetable in 'Me-Time' so I can re-identity with myself, or time alone with my partner, and get that reminder in that I'm Not Just a Mummy. When I'm with my children, I'm fully there. When it's about me, I'll fully there too. Compartmentalised living works for me. Yes, you might have to get up that extra hour earlier and go to bed that extra hour late, but it is worth it.

The next time you feel like you've got far too much on that to do list, too many people asking for your support and a bucket full of household chores to do, sit back and ask your mind and body if you need some time out or if you can delegate. Can you ask your partner to take over? Are your children old enough to understand the concept of chores and carry them out? You're not the only one who lives in the house, so why should you be the only one expected to clean it? Plus teaching your children how to clean up after themselves, take responsibility for their own homework and make a sandwich shows that you are preparing them on how to be independent. Everyone will understand that you're overloaded and respect your honesty. And with this support you'll eventually feel like you can do everything you need to do.

Chapter Twenty Five

Seriously, Did They Say That?

"From being a vegetarian throughout pregnancy to working out at the gym three days over my due date, I had quite a lot of looks and judgement from day one, but the second I found out I was pregnant (which was a complete shock) I decided I would always maintain me. I probably became quite defiant in trying to prove people wrong, and every "you can't do that..." just spurred me on to do it even more, especially when it came to the topic of travelling like I used to before I became a mum...why couldn't I? Six months on and more hurdles are met. The pressure of weaning to guidelines the older generation don't understand (and the word stupid being used when I refused to introduce solids until 6 months). The pressures from work when I changed my maternity from 6 to 9 months (and the guilt and stress that followed), but I will always follow my instinct because nothing is right or wrong, it is what works for you and makes YOU happy." Sarah

Through the traditional media, and even more so with social media, we have created this virtual bond with celebrities as if we know them personally. A lot of people believe everything they see or hear, even when it sounds so false. It's a trust we have embedded into the celebrity title. This is why celebrities have become so influential across the world.

A few years ago, I came across an article about the model Chrissy Teigen. She had gone out not long after her baby was born and received a lot of backlash. Surely women can decide when they're ready to move out of the house? We all recover differently. Another headline that shocked me was reading that Kim Kardashian was having a breakdown over not getting her body back into shape post-birth. It didn't come across as a real article with Kim's actual words and the pictures were of her eating an ice cream, as though the media were taunting her. I always wonder how celebrities like these two ladies cope with the stress that comes with media headlines about their parenting styles or body image, surely it must be tough.

I grew up in the era of the Spice Girls. They were the 'in' image of what women looked and behaved like. To me, each Spice Girl represented a different personality, especially with the clothes they wore. I loved the diversity of the five ladies. Their words, girl power image, behaviour and powerful choices filled me with hope that the world was accepting about who you are and your beliefs. It wasn't until my own motherhood journey began that I realised that the girl power message isn't always accepted or welcomed.

In my early motherhood years I would read about celebrity mothers who have amazing careers, marry into true love and have the most beautiful children who always look like they are super behaved. But then the media rip this apart with other stories of true love marriages spiralling into affairs, separations and legal battles. And they also change the goal posts on what is acceptable. Beyonce's daughter has made headlines for being very sassy and strong minded. A few years earlier that would have been naughty behaviour. It's all very personal and, being truthful, I don't know if the celebrity status is worth the amount of insight and opinion the world has on your life.

The media makes us all ask harmful questions that threaten to undermine our identities. Your life becomes a world of 'why'? Why don't you look like that after having your baby? Why doesn't your hair grow like that? Why doesn't your relationship look like theirs?

What I suggest doing is to remember that there are two sides to every story, every photo and every online post. Being yourself should be seen as a gift. You're unique and offer something different to the world.

But how can we separate what's real and what isn't? Number one is to think about if what you're reading has a purpose in helping you on your journey. Can it help you personally become happy while remaining who you are? Number two is to think about how this is not your concern and no longer allow these thoughts to flow into your mind and take over your energy and focus. This is challenging at first, but like any life lesson, once it's taught and established, it will make a difference to your life.

Chapter Twenty Six

Escape from the Daily Routine

"You can get sick of walking in the same park every day, eating the same meals day in and day out and having to make all of the decisions." Robyn

I understand the struggle that comes with not feeling content with your daily routine. It can seem like motherhood is pretty boring from the outside, and sometimes you can feel a little bit bored on the inside too. You might be tempted to do something drastic like moving house, changing careers or leaving a partner. This can appear to be the only option to make you feel better and make the situation, experience or past disappear. I'm sorry to break it to you, but running away from whatever it is that's making you feel these emotions, especially self-doubt, can't and won't disappear with a new postcode, job or partner.

It's like when you're in a relationship that isn't working. You might think that having a baby can heal betrayal, unhappiness and trust issues, like I did. My second child was a beautiful surprise and from the relationship struggles I was experiencing, like betrayal in the form of an affair, I did think that she would bring clarity to my partner. That part didn't work out for me, even though I did get two amazing children, who I am truly grateful for.

Not being content with how you are living your life can destroy your confidence. This also takes away the motivation to make changes. From working with a lot of women over the past two years, I have noticed that most were having these negative, masked feelings because they found that they weren't being true to who they were through their behaviour, actions or relationships. Have you ever experienced that uneasy feeling of not knowing what to do in a situation, so you do something completely out of character? I have plenty of times!

Imagine sitting on a bus going to a job that you don't feel is taking you in the direction of the success you had once envisioned. Or you are going to see a partner in relationship that isn't meeting your expectations. Both can make you feel like you're living life in 'eat, sleep ,repeat' mode. What can you do or what do you need to make the changes to shift these current feelings? We all have this energy and strength within us that allows us to overcome the negative situations, thoughts and behaviours. Think about it like this, the desire to change equals the amount of change that is needed. To me that meant I had to be the source of the change. I wanted to feel like me again. I wanted to take back control. I started small, but I built the strength up every day to make bigger changes to overcome the challenges that were holding me back from living my life in full control. Eventually, I got off that bus. I left that relationship.

To pull yourself out of an environment that you have been in for so long can feel daunting. Even just thinking about escaping your daily routine, the people that surround you, a partner and any negativity that is currently making you have these unwanted feelings can, at times, be unimaginable. If I said it was easy I would be lying.

But you are the answer to your happiness. Stop the constant questioning of yourself and your life. This drains you of the energy needed to start shifting those thoughts to positive.

Recognise the barriers that are restricting you. As I have referred to in this book several times, writing a diary or a journal which includes your daily routine and the feelings that surround each action, behaviour and person who you spend time with, will help you come to the realisation on areas that you need to challenge.

Once you are deep into writing your journal or diary you will start to notice the patterns that you can then break down and commit time to changing.

Be open minded and communicate with your own thoughts, filter out any negativity and train your mind into not allowing more to follow in. Be wise with who you spend your days with and make sure you're putting your own needs as a priority, by choosing not to be around people who intoxicate you with their own negativity. You do have that choice.

Chapter Twenty Seven

Don't Forget About You

You need to get out more
It's not healthy for you or the baby
You need some time to yourself
If you wanted to, then you would find the time
I'm sure you can write your own list of opinions and advice that was directed at you during pregnancy and motherhood.

Most of the time it's advice from friends, family and professionals intended to give you more knowledge. It's given as a sign of support, and when worded correctly, can make a massive different to how you feel during pregnancy and motherhood. But it can feel like an attack.

It's only natural that the people close to you want to support you through what can become a challenging journey. No matter how strong your character or personality is, the changes, feelings and shifts in your pattern can overcome the strength, and leave you feeling weak and vulnerable.
Feeling like this can become noticeable to friends and family, who can automatically assume that your new-found emotions and behaviours are because you're not coping with pregnancy or motherhood. But I think we all cope, even through the most challenging times. The best advice we could all receive would be, 'don't forget about yourself.'

When I had my first baby, it was difficult to remember who I was because motherhood was taking me away from the path society expects from someone who is barely out of their teens.

Everyone around me was at university or working full time, going out over the weekends and basically having all of the 'Me Time' that they wanted. Did I envy them? Yes, I guess at the time I did. Do I envy them now? Not at all. My children are growing up beautiful and I'm a very proud mother. But that time when I did envy them was because I forgot about myself. I kept listening to who I was 'supposed' to be at that age. The real truth is that we can do anything we want to, when we want to.

You can find yourself thinking about the things you can't do now that you're pregnant or a mother. It's easily done, and it doesn't mean you're a terrible person, or a terrible mother. You are just remembering you.

You could try sharing stories about the 'Me Time' you experienced to your children before they came along. It's natural and it teaches them about who their mother was and, most importantly, who their mum is.

Chapter Twenty Eight

Moving Forward

"I remember coming home after my shower party, overwhelmed by the gifts for my new baby. I was so happy until the room was silent and I realised that even though I had a lot of support from my friends outside my home, that I didn't have anyone to come home to that I could share my excitement with. My husband passed away when I was two months pregnant and I was reminded of this with a quiet house, until our son was born and now my home is never empty." Jess

Moving forward and staying focused on you and your identity while looking after a family is hard. But remember in motherhood, no matter what your circumstances are, you are never alone.

My advice would be to stop comparing yourself to others, and remember these simple points:

Motherhood doesn't have to be the only thing you enjoy. Release the guilt about having your own time and enjoying it. Chances are you will still be thinking of your children when you spend time away from them, that's natural. But you can enjoy these thoughts and remind yourself that you are bringing them up well.

Becoming a mother doesn't mean you stop enjoying the things you like to do. You will need to adjust. You can't go out all night, every night, but you can find ways of having fun that suit your new identity.

Open up your heart to self-love and acceptance. You deserve to be loved as a woman.

We have those daily struggles when it seems like our world is crashing down around us. We battle through those times even when we don't believe there is going to be a positive outcome.

We remind ourselves that we do it for our children, when we should also want to overcome those times for ourselves as well. There should be no shame in saying that you want to get through struggles or that you want to achieve new goals for yourself.

I've had to face a lot of these daily struggles where staying in bed seemed like the better option at the time. I remember waking up a few weeks after my relationship with my children's dad had ended and I knew it was time to face the challenge of telling people the truth about why it ended and how I was in a better place. This was despite feeling (wrongly) embarrassed to be a single mum. I allowed people to give me their advice on how I was going to survive and I moved forward taking each day as it came.

Driving yourself forward doesn't mean pushing all of the fear to one side. Fear doesn't automatically disappear when it's asked to. It takes time, confidence, belief and trust. These are qualities that haven't always come easy for you. This is not because we don't want to have all of those skills and qualities, it's because there are so many barriers and obstacles that we are challenged with on a daily basis.

Chapter Twenty Nine

A Mum with a Plan

"For a long time I suffered from identity loss. It wasn't until my children left home that I realised I was lost without them. I don't just mean I missed my children, I didn't know what to do with myself. I didn't even know what food to buy for myself." Pamela

Having a plan isn't so bad, right? So, what's stopping you from creating a life-focused one to support the re-creation of your thoughts pattern, and to keep at hand for when you start to believe and feel that some areas in your life aren't doing so good?

I use a weekly structured timetable as mine. I write out where I need to be and what I'm there for. I start every day with morning affirmations or listening to a short positive audio to set me up for the day ahead. I plan the small and big goals that I want to achieve into my actions, because I know it's the small steps that will create the goals. A little bit of structure can be like pixie dust, as my daughter would say.

Waking up every day with a vision board, whether it's your family vision board that you have all created together or the more personal vision board for yourself, will help you see the steps of action you need. This is for you and should be true to everything that you believe. Allowing yourself to open up to these changes will support you with contentment with everything that you do and everything that happens around you.

My own board works as a visual version of my goals list. I cut out images of the things that I would like to see happen in the future. My current vision board for the next six months includes the outcome I would like from The Not Just a Mummy Platform, my next holiday destination and a picture of my family, looking healthy and happy. Your board has to be visible in your family home for you all to be constantly reminded of the vision that you created together.

Creating your own family vision board can be a fun activity and doesn't have to be made complicated; it's something that all the family will enjoy getting involved in. It doesn't require lots of money to create. I used an A3 canvas from a local store.

I then asked the children and my husband what they would like to have this time next year that we don't have enough of now. It nearly broke me when my son replied with 'more family time'. But we work on that a lot now and it gave me even more energy to make my business a success and plan my time better.

A must do bit of advice: Allow the children to cut out even if it doesn't look perfect to you. Let them decorate it and have a real input. You can't create a vision board for your family without it being a project designed by you all.
It's only when you begin to put all of the puzzle pieces back together, that you start to feel and react differently. It's like waking up from a dream that seemed like it was never going to end, a massive breath of fresh air that you should mindfully appreciate.

Welcome yourself back because you've been missed by your inner woman. Now you have to keep driving yourself forward with your mindful, positive new attitude and never let anyone throw that duvet of doubt over your feelings and thoughts.

Chapter Thirty

Welcome Back

"Mummy life is a rollercoaster , every turn is different for every mother but the end can be as rewarding as each other's, you just need to hold on tight and ask to slow down when it goes too fast." Grace

Starting to feel a little bit more like yourself? I hope so! I can't promise you that you won't have days when you feel that things are slipping out of your hands, but don't let this dishearten you or disrupt your future plans. It happens and it's in those moments that you need to be realistic with yourself and believe that it's okay and you've got this. You can have this faith because you are mindfully aware of what's going on and you'll be surprised just how much you gain back that control.

 I will say it again - be your own biggest cheerleader! Don't waste your energy or time worrying about what everybody else is or isn't doing. Instead focus all of that energy on yourself, your family and the people in your life who deserve you. Your mind will never be still with peace, unless you give it the time and rest that it deserves.

It's perfectly fine to have ambition when you have children. I meet and speak with women from all over the world, who all believe that their drive and passion comes from wanting to make their children proud. I agree that the extra push comes from this and wanting the best for your children. But I also believe that every woman should want to hit those life goals for herself. There is no selfishness in wanting this, and to have that feel good, positive feeling of accomplishment. Success will differ from woman to woman; everyone has their own vision of what success means to them. Ask yourself, what does this mean to you? If you were to reach your own level of success, what would change in your life? How would it make you feel?

One of the most important lessons I have learned both in life and in motherhood is that when you surround yourself with like-minded, positive women, it does increase your own positivity towards everything you do.

I have two choices when listening to the words and past experiences of others; I can either relive it with them and feel their hurt (this will feel like I'm sitting on an emotional roundabout in a cold, dark environment basically turning around and not getting anywhere) or I can support them with taking their first steps on how to live in the present, by encouraging peace and acceptance for everything that they have experienced.

The hard times happened in the past. This does entitle you to feel all of the emotions that you're feeling, but bringing the past into your present moment only allows it to take the lead, walking in front of your future. You become unable to create your own vision, as your past takes control and maps it out for you.

Our behaviour, choices and actions all have an effect on the people who surround us, the people who love us and who we also love. This is not what we intend to do, but without reaching out for support this is sadly what can happen and even the strongest of characters can feel affected.

Believing in change is the first step to moving forward. A mindful dose of clarity of who you are and what you believe in can create the right shift. This is possible, and you get to decide what you want to achieve. Nobody else can determine how much drive, passion and energy that you are going to commit to your vision.

The positive energy that you create from your own thoughts, behaviours and actions will shift the energy that exists in your environment, pushing away the negative, making you feel lifted from self-doubt, worry and anxiety.

During mum and toddler sessions, I often get talking to other mums. We shared so many helpful stories about our children's sleep patterns, routine, feeding etc but hardly ever our own needs. But recently I've noticed this changing. With the ten-year gap between my two girls, I have seen that society is finally allowing mums to talk about the difficult sides of raising children. No one is getting it all right, all of the time.

Getting into a healthy mindset is a steady process, that we all measure in different ways, unique to each individual. I'm lucky with my circle of friends, but I have built up this group during the process of defining my identity. Some days we meet up and let off steam about things in our life. That's completely normal, and in my opinion, it's healthy. Yes, we have days when we may have forgotten to get Mrs Positive out of bed, but that's life and the sooner we wake up to the reality that emotions create feelings and feelings create behaviours then we're fine.

After speaking out about my own identity experiences, I started to receive messages from other women in my community and across the world who had all experienced similar thoughts, feelings and behaviour. They all agreed that it's far too easy to hide away from the world than it is to stand up and face the reality that is becoming a mother.

Moving forward and taking your identity with you, will be a blessing in itself. You'll start to notice a massive difference in how you approach situations and how you choose to move past them. If you're wanting to be that change you have to allow yourself to be a priority without any shame. Treat yourself like you would treat others, starting with conditioning and nurturing your mind to show love, compassion, empathy and trust to your thoughts, feelings and words.

You have probably heard of the saying 'trust your gut feeling'. I strongly believe this is true. Don't let anyone influence your thoughts, feelings, words or behaviours through their own. Take the control, feel the control and move forward into a happy, content, positive environment full of opportunities that are waiting for you.

You are Not Just a Mummy. You're a real human with feelings, needs and desires. You are a strong woman, with a fleet of empowering women by your side. You are inspirational, strong and deserve to live your life to the full, without having to feel guilty about every thought, decision and move that you make. You should never feel like you have to be someone else to please everyone else. Keep your eyes wide open and stay in control of the path that you want to be on. If you start to see yourself swaying don't panic! You've noticed and that's how you will get right back on track.

You have my word and my promise that I will forever be here for any women who need to connect. You are not alone.
Much Love
Clare - Not Just a Mummy x

Special Thank You:

My children, to me you are the world. There is never a day that goes by that I don't appreciate every waking moment that I get to share with you.

My husband, thank you for all of your support, even when the road wasn't clear enough to see, you kept walking down it with me. I am forever grateful that I have you in my life. Thank you for loving me for who I am.

My mum, you showed me through the love you have for me, how to be the mother I am today. Thank you for being my guide.

My siblings, you all played a massive part in my journey and all added to it with your own uniqueness. Kay, you brighten up even my darkest days when I didn't feel like I deserved the title of mum. Jo, you took me under your wing and gave me the strength I needed to move forward. Paul, you protected my mind when I needed you most. Thomas, you inspire me every day with the courage you have to stand up for what you believe in. Lee, you motivated me to understand that fitness strength comes from having a strong mind. Daniel, you made me happy with how much you looked up to me.

My dad and Janet, for always listening to my crazy visions and encouraging me to go for them!

My mother and father in law, thank you for welcoming me into your family and always being there for me.

Clare Coombes, for believing in my vision, encouraging me to keep going and always being there when I needed support.

Nicola Lowe, for creating such a powerful image for the Not Just a Mummy front illustration.

My amazing family who I wouldn't change for the world!

My friends, thank you for bringing so much inspiration into my life and adding so many new chapters to my journey.

And finally a special thank you to me, for never giving up!

Always here

Clare Bowers

Facebook - Not Just A Mummy

Instagram - Notjustamummy_world

Email - **clare@notjustamummyworld.co.uk**

Stay connected by subscribing to the Not Just a Mummy website.
www.notjustamummyworld.co.uk

Printed in Great Britain
by Amazon